Read And Pray

Spiritual Growth Study Guide
*Understanding Salvation
*Sharing Jesus
*Grief Relief
*Life as a Christian

Dr. Brenda Kendrick

- Published by Kendle Direct Publishing. Copyright material first print 2024. Available on Amazon.
- Scripture quotes are from the King James Version, or New King James Version unless otherwise noted. Some names and places may be changed to protect the privacy of individuals.

RAP = Read And Pray

Dedicated:
To God's glory
To advance His kingdom

Appreciation:

Thanks to Rev. Jeff Allred and Rev. Don Graham my pastors
for their wisdom in leadership and contributing an outline of sermons.
(See page 205 for Bro. Jeff's message and page 108 for Bro. Don's message.)
Thanks to Chayne Childers for his encouragement to put this material to print..

Special thanks to my husband Dennis Kendrick for
always being patient and kind while supporting me
during the many hours in putting this material together.

In loving memory of my late husband/pastor, Dale Hyche,
who preached Jesus as The Way, The Truth and The Life for forty-five years.

RAP = Read And Pray

Table of Contents

Page 6 Introduction & Objective

Page 11 Chapter 1 - Charts

Page 55 Chapter 2 - Reading The Bible

Page 73 Chapter 3 – Understanding Salvation

Page 93 Chapter 4 - Prayer

Page 119 Chapter 5 - Sharing Jesus

Page 135 Chapter 6 - Grief Relief

Page 169 Chapter 7 - Life As A Christian

<u>*Reconciliation I need it.*</u>
(You & me lost)
<u>*Justification He did it.*</u>
(You &Me saved)
<u>*Sanctification He is doing it.*</u>
(You & Me learning to live holy in an unholy world)
<u>*Glorification He will do it.*</u>
(You & Me living holy in a holy world - heaven)

Page 214 Summary -The Main Things:

RAP = Read And Pray

"In the beginning God created
the heaven and the earth."
Genesis 1:1

RAP = Read And Pray

"In the beginning was the Word,
and the Word was with God,
and the Word was God"
John 1:1

RAP = Read And Pray

Introduction

The R.A.P. (READ and PRAY) material herein was originally put together by pencil on paper before it was typed on a manual typewriter then later entered into a word processor. Section One was created in the early 1970's shortly after my husband started pastoring his first church. We were young, almost penniless and suddenly we were trying to teach when we still needed to be taught. Printed materials were costly and at that time our church could only afford Sunday School books. God laid it upon my heart to create a simple study guide that would encourage churchwide participation with Bible reading being the main focus. The best way to do that was to encourage individual Bible study straight from the Word of God. The Holy Spirit would be the one responsible for counsel and guidance and our involvement is to watch Him work in our lives as well as His Church.

Thus, RAP Sessions were birthed. These reading and praying sessions took on a life of their own with people reading the entire Bible (every verse of it) instead of playing bible-bingo with one verse here and one verse there. It dawned on me that Christians really do want to know what the Bible is all about but have no clue where to start. I chose particular subjects for memorization and tried to lace them with importance in understanding how God has always been in control and how He has always loved His people. From scribing the Ten Commandments to Moses, to the calling of His twelve disciples He has always had a divine plan for humanity. In today's society that divine plan is fuzzy to the point of distortion as we approach His second coming. It is more vital than ever that His people understand He is the same yesterday, today and forevermore and His loving grace alone will bring help, hope and healing.

Understanding the Bible begins at the point of salvation because with salvation comes the Holy Spirit's indwelling counsel. The Bible is a mystery but understandable to those that seek revelation through faith in Jesus Christ. Once saved by grace, the Holy Spirit will guide the believer to spiritual growth as well as correct those who have been misguided by faulty thinking. To walking successful in this world, investment must be made by each individual because spiritual growth requires personal discipline, sacrifice of time and commitment. The benefits will far outweigh any sacrifices.

Those who start running without having a visualization of the track will stumble at the hurdles, but those who desire fellowship with God will begin the race with a desire to keep their eyes on the checkered flag and not the stumbling blocks.

This study guide has seven sections and a summary. The charts in section one are developed to be self-explanatory and come with a purpose. I suggest enlisting a friend or small group to dive into these basic facts that even some seasoned Christian do not know. Having a knowledge of where to find things in your Bible is very important. The *Concordance* at the back of your Bible is a very good reference for finding Scriptures to either back up opinions as truth or condemn them as unscriptural.

I've found one consistency in every church of that I have been a member. That being: the lack of teaching basic Bible 101 and discipleship, from the cradle to the casket. We are born with a need-to-know God's Word and should be ever-learning until the day we die. Every beginning has a start. Today it is possible to open your phone and read the Bible, but I do not suggest reading the Bible on your phone unless you are a very disciplined individual who will not be tempted or distracted to open social media for a quick-look. Using a Bible permits one to make notes in the margin or highlight certain passages for quick reference for another time.

RAP = Read And Pray

God loves to participate when He sees someone reading the printed Bible and He may nudge you with a special nugget of revelation that He wants you to claim. It is a delight to God when He sees and hears us *praying the Scripture,* that you will be guided to do during this study.

The Apostle Paul used his imprisonments to write letters that would go on to be included in the Bible because they were inspired by the Holy Spirit. These letters are God's words as if God spoke them directly to me and you; because He did speak them directly to Paul. Then Paul transcribed them verbatim in order for God to share them with us two thousand years after the fact. The key to reading the Bible is to listen to God as if He is speaking in your ear. When we speak back to God in prayer we create a unity with Him. That unity becomes relationship, and that relationship becomes fellowship with our Father in heaven.

In His Word you will find healing, hope, freedom, liberty, satisfaction, peace, and joy in daily living. Being a Christian is so much more than security of missing hell. Being a Chrisitan is joy unspeakable and full of glory for the here and now.

How can I make such a claim? Because (1) nothing heals like God's Word and (2) Jesus Christ is the Great Physician. When a person concentrates on these two things the result will be astonishingly beneficial to one's mental health, physical wellbeing and spiritual security.

It has been said by an anonymous writer that: "In the throne room of the Almighty, we get perspective, and we will walk out a lot lighter than we were when we came in. Prayer has a way of centering our lives on what is eternal rather than worst-case scenarios and self-conceived doom." There is more to life than abundant how-to commercialize self-help books. This is not meant to be one of those books.

As you will notice on the content page of this book there are many topics discussed. Topics that I have discovered over a lifetime that will positively shape a person when understood by revelation of the Holy Spirit. My advice is to get your Bible, open it prayerfully and receive it literally. To aid this process, it would be beneficial to have an accountability partner or team who will support you as you support them in daily efforts to complete each task. Take time to research, and before long you will desire more and more of God's Word because you have a hunger for truth and *God's truth* will stand all the way to the end of the ages.

Let's say a person is satisfied with only reading the New Testament because the New Covenant teaches us that we live under grace that has been allowed since the ultimate sacrifice was given through the New Testament and by the life, death and resurrection of Jesus Christ, the Messiah. Therefore if a person thinks that the Old Testament is not worth studying it would be like having jewels; but no treasure chest to put them in. Like having furniture; but no house. Like having God; but no heaven.

Without knowing the Old Testament truths we would:

(1) *Miss the prophecies*: So then, how would we know they were fulfilled in Christ Jesus?
(2) *Deny miracles of yesteryears*: So then, If miracles happened a long time ago, and if God is the same God now as He was then; what keeps miracles from happening today in your own life?

RAP = Read And Pray

The answers to both these questions center around God and God's existence as the Creator of all things. First, how could prophecies exist without knowledge of yesterday, today and tomorrow's events? Only the Trinity of God has been, is and always will be present in all time. Therefore only God (evident in The Trinity of God the Father, Jesus Christ the Son. and The Holy Spirit) was here, is here and will be here for all eternity to *predict and fulfill* prophecy. Secondly, *God provides and proofs* miracles of past, present and future. Miracles have been documented and proven by evidence throughout history and present day. The only thing that remains is the fulfillment of prophecies for the future that are found in future revelation in the Book of Revelation as the last book of the Bible. (You will not understand any of this unless you are a believer of the true Gospel of Jesus Christ. Therefore seek and pray for understanding of this Gospel. This understand is the purpose of this study and only found in the pages of the book called The Holy Bible.)

The Old Testament is full of *"thus saith The Lord's"* as well as tremendous miracles of deliverance for God's people; So then, thinking that the Old Testament has no place in today's world is just plain faulty thinking. In studying The Holy Bible – we must include *all* of it.

I chose to use Malachi chapter 3 as the final context in this introduction because therein there is tremendous truths for current day. <u>First</u>, our **GOD has not changed**, His Word doesn't need to be upload week after week with the latest and greatest. It began with the latest and greatest and will continue to be so. He is the same yesterday, today, and forevermore. <u>Second</u>, He says we have robbed Him. We better pay attention to that statement. We rob God not just because we do not faithfully deposit money-tithe into an offering plate; but also because we do not invest 10% of our time toward serving Him. I've done the math for you. That is 16.8 hours each week that should be dedicated to God. Who does that? <u>Thirdly</u>, gathering together in God's House (church) with other believers is not only a good idea, but also a promised way for petitions to be answered when God's people are seeking Him through prayer together, and in person.

Therefore the purpose of this book is not an easy-out or popular course of study but it is to encourage you to learn the truth for yourself by Reading God's Word and communicating with Him in prayer. He is the One who wants fellowship with you, every single day. You will not find satisfaction for your soul's desire in this book or because of this study guide in your hand right now. You will find satisfaction for your soul, in the Word of God, Prayer and fellowship with your Creator.

Malachi 3
v. 6 – "For I am the Lord, I change not; therefore ye sons of Jacob are not consumed."
v. 8 – "Will a man rob God? Yet ye have robbed me. But ye say,
Wherein have we robbed thee? In tithes and offerings."
v. 9 – "Ye are cursed with a curse: for ye have robbed me, even this whole nation."
v. 16 – "Then they that feared the Lord spake often one to another: and the Lord harkened, and heard it, and a book of remembrance was written before Him for them
that feared the Lord, and that thought upon His name."
v. 17 – "And they shall be mine, saith the Lord of hosts, in that day when I make up my jewels;
and I will spare them, as a man spareth his own son that serveth him."
v. 18 – "Then shall ye return, and discern between the righteous and the wicked,
between him that serveth God and him that serveth Him not."

RAP = Read And Pray

Objective

The first objective is for the reader to begin a daily Bible reading and prayer time that will result in an intimate communication and fellowship with God. Then as a result of spending time with God, the reader will have a desire to learn Bible basics beginning with the memorizing of the 66 books of the Bible. This will enable you to locate scriptures faster when following along with the pastor as he mentions passages during his sermons.

Other basic knowledge will include memorizing the 10 commandments, twelve disciples, and twelve tribes of Israel, etc. These fact are listed in a point system to keep tract of progress. This is for your own personal use as a motivation to gage consistency. As you progress through this study new material can be introduced on an individual basis as you work at your own speed.

In the past when we conducted RAP sessions at numerous churches we used the point system by dividing participants into two teams, they were known as the Hallelujah team and the Amen team. At the end of a set time, usually 6 to 10 weeks, the winning team with the most points would be treated by the other team to a social of some sort. Usually most people enjoy some degree of healthy competition that will be rewarded. In this study, you will challenge yourself and the reward is eternally beneficial because the motive is more fellowship with God.

Each challenge is referred to as a session. For example, learning the Romans road to salvation is a session. Studying the twelve tribes of Israel is a session, etc. You may go as slowly or fast throughout this study as your time allows. I suggest you look over the following pages and get an overview of the material and then decide that challenge you want to start first. For instance, if you already can quote all 66 books of the Bible – then do that and log your points.

Be Verbel – Speak The Bible

Don't be shy in quoting the things you learn out loud to a person on your team or even your children as you drive them to school. Write your favorite verses on index cards to memorize and quote them several times a day, even while showering or cooking dinner. This excites God and causes stress to the old devil, and we certainly win battles when we back him into the corner with God's Word. When resisted he leaves the premises. He cannot stand in God's presence. As you become familiar with this simple approach to Bible Study you may invite others to join your circle and work together, as a family or even a neighborhood activity. Prayerfully consider joining with another person who can be your accountability partner.

For me, the most important part has always been getting a person to actually open the Bibles in their homes as a regular daily activity. Sooner or later, you will read something that rings your bell, and new ideas and thoughts will come pouring into your mind, as if you have never read it before. That is the work of the Holy Spirit. Invite Him to guide you through these sessions.

Do the few simple things and then you will dig deeper and advance to Promises, Parables, Prophecies, etc. At the beginning of each class I encourage people to start their Bible study *at the Beginning* – being Genesis. Genesis actually means "the beginning". Couple reading Genesis with either Psalms or one of the Gospels. In order to understand the rest of the Bible, you must understand Genesis. And you can rack up quite a few points by reading the book of Genesis!

RAP = Read And Pray

Another important thing to remember in getting off to a great start in your spiritual growth is to concentrate on learning to use the concordance found in the back of almost every Bible. Practice looking up Scripture by using key words to locate the book, chapter and verse where a particular quote is found. Get familiar with how to use references to locate favorite verses or helpful verses for any situation where you need God to speak to you.

Challenges bring possibilities and rewards previously thought to be impossible. Invest in this challenge and you will surprise yourself. One lady who had not read her Bible in many years because of declining eyesight decided to try anyway. Once she started reading she found out it was still possible with larger print and she read the entire Bible that year. She said: "the more I read, the more I wanted to read." She just had to start.

*"Lord, teach us to search the Scriptures;
for in them we have eternal life:
and they testify of You. Then
You will open our understanding,
that we might understand the scriptures."
(John 5:39 and Luke 24:45)*

Chapter 1

Group & Individual Charts

RAP = Read And Pray

JUMP START PAGE

Since *reading and praying* are the keys to spiritual growth, we will start by praying and reading right off this first page. First read from your Bible the scripture listed below and write out the Scriptures on the lines provided. Next pray the Scripture as shown in the example provided, using verses that speak to your heart. This will put you off and running on your journey of learning Bible basics for life.

This guidebook is not a race, it's a journey.

Throughout this study guide you will find a Journal The Scriptures page and a Prayer Chart for the purpose of updating your request with praise reports. Use the next page now to get started and pray for God in order to: 1. Open your mind and heart to hear Him through His Word. 2. Ask Him to help you understand the Scripture. 3. Ask God to direct you with His divine will to grow spiritually.

Write the Scriptures below:

Write out Philippians 4:4-8

_____
_____
_____
_____
_____
_____

Praying the Scripture Example:

Pray: Lord God, I Have been very anxious about life lately so now I'm giving you those concerns in prayer and thanksgiving because I desire the peace you promise that passes all understanding. I want you to keep my heart and my mind through Christ Jesus. Help me think on things that are true, honest, just, pure and lovely. I will think on things that are of a good report and righteous. Thank you Father for your promises. Amen.

_____

To complete this exercise:
Choose one of the following Scriptures to write out both the Scripture and your Prayer:
Psalms 118:24, Psalms 19:14 or Philippians 4:13

_____
_____

Prayer:_____
_____
_____

Now give yourself a hug – You Can Do This!

There will be "bonus points" pages throughout this study guide. Hunt them out for extra points. (Bonus points = 500 page)

RAP = Read And Pray

Prayer Record

Date:	Request:	Answer:
	Open my heart to hear you speak to me from your Word.	

Date:	Request:	Answer:
	Help me understand the Scriptures.	

Date:	Request:	Answer:
	Guide me to grow spiritually every day.	

(Bonus points = 500 page)

"Lord, teach us to <u>search</u> the scriptures;
for in them we have eternal life:
and they testify of You.
Then You will open our understanding,
that we might understand the scriptures."
(John 5:39 and Luke 24:45)

RAP = Read And Pray

Attendance Chart for Facilitator

The facilitator chooses Team Captains and Captains recruit members.
(Try to choose evenly challenging per team number of participants & strengths.)

Name:	Week 1	Week 2	Week 3	Week 4	Week 5	Week 6	Week 7	Week 8
1.								
2.								
3.								
4.								
5.								
6.								
7.								
8.								
9.								
10.								
11.								
12.								
13.								
14.								
15.								
16.								
17.								
18.								
19.								
20.								
21.								
22.								
23.								
24.								
25.								
26.								
27.								
28.								
29.								
30.								

RAP = Read And Pray

TALLY SHEET FOR TEAM CHAPTAINS

*Bible verses read during the week.	One point each
Memorize a chapter (at least 5 consecutive verses) Add 50 points for each additional verse.	1000 points
Memorize the books of Old Testament (See page 65)	2000 points
Memorize the books of New Testament (See page 65)	1000 points
10 Commandments (See page 25)	500 points
12 Disciples (See page 29)	500 points
12 Tribes of Israel (See page 35)	500 points
Written bonus sheets are inserted throughout this study guide. Be sure to hunt them out.	500 points each

Amen Team

TOTAL FOR TEAM PER WEEK	Week #1	Week #2	Week #3	Week #4	Week #5	Week #6	Week #7	Week #8	TOTAL
Present 500 points BIBLE READING									
Memory Verses									
Quote N.T. Books									
Quote O.T. Books									
Quote 10 Commandments									
Quote 12 Disciples									
Quote 12 Tribes									
BONUS SHEETS (X 500 each)									
OTHER POINTS									

RAP = Read And Pray

TALLY SHEET FOR TEAM CHAPTAIN

*Bible verses read during the week.	One point each
Memorize a chapter (at least 5 consecutive verses) Add 50 points for each additional verse.	1000 points
Memorize the books of Old Testament (See page 65)	2000 points
Memorize the books of New Testament (See page 65)	1000 points
10 Commandments (See page 25)	500 points
12 Disciples (See page 29)	500 points
12 Tribes of Israel (See page 35)	500 points
Written bonus sheets (See pages 46-48, 50-53)	500 points each

Hallelujah Team

TOTAL FOR TEAM PER WEEK	Week #1	Week #2	Week #3	Week #4	Week #5	Week #6	Week #7	Week #8	TOTAL
Present 500 Points									
BIBLE READING									
Memory Verses									
Quote N.T. Books									
Quote O.T. Books									
Quote 10 Commandments									
Quote 12 Disciples									
Quote 12 Tribes									
BONUS SHEETS (X 500 each)									
OTHER POINTS									

RAP = Read And Pray

Charts For Personal Use

RAP = Read And Pray

TALLY SHEET

*Bible verses read during the week.	One point each
Memorize a chapter (at least 5 consecutive verses) Add 50 points for each additional verse.	1000 points
Memorize the books of Old Testament (See page 65)	2000 points
Memorize the books of New Testament (See page 65)	1000 points
10 Commandments (See page 25)	500 points
12 Disciples (See page 29)	500 points
12 Tribes of Israel (See page 35)	500 points
Written bonus sheets (See pages 46-48, 50-53)	500 points each

BONUS
Read entire New Testament (7,957) Receive 10,000 extra points

	Week #1	Week #2	Week #3	Week #4	Week #5	Week #6	Week #7	Week #8	TOTAL
BIBLE READING									
Memory Verses									
Quote O.T. Books									
Quote N.T. Books									
10 Commandments									
12 Disciples									
12 Tribes									
BONUS SHEETS (X 500 each)									

Read entire Old Testament (23,145)- Add 30,000 extra points

CONGRATULATIONS! YOU DID IT!
Grand total for 8-week sessions _____

RAP = Read And Pray

Personal Bible Reading Tally Charts

BIBLE READING CHART – WEEK One						
Beginning Date:				Verses Total for **Week One**:		
Sunday	Monday	Tuesday	Wednesday	Thursday	Friday	Saturday

BIBLE READING CHART – WEEK TWO						
Beginning Date:				Verses Total for **Week Two**:		
Sunday	Monday	Tuesday	Wednesday	Thursday	Friday	Saturday

BIBLE READING CHART – WEEK THREE						
Beginning Date:				Verses Total for **Week Three**:		
Sunday	Monday	Tuesday	Wednesday	Thursday	Friday	Saturday

BIBLE READING CHART – WEEK FOUR						
Beginning Date:				Verses Total for **Week Four:**		
Sunday	Monday	Tuesday	Wednesday	Thursday	Friday	Saturday

Pray The Scriptures
(John 5:39 and Luke 24:45)

"Lord, teach us to "Search the scriptures; for in them
we have eternal life: and they testify of You.
Then You will open our understanding,
that we might understand the scriptures."

RAP = Read And Pray

BIBLE REAING CHART – WEEK FIVE							
Beginning Date:				Verses Total for **Week Five**:			
Sunday	Monday	Tuesday	Wednesday	Thursday	Friday	Saturday	

BIBLE READING CHART – WEEK SIX							
Beginning Date:				Verses Total for **Week Six:**			
Sunday	Monday	Tuesday	Wednesday	Thursday	Friday	Saturday	

BIBLE READING CHART – WEEK SEVEN							
Beginning Date:				Verses Total for **Week Seven**:			
Sunday	Monday	Tuesday	Wednesday	Thursday	Friday	Saturday	

BIBLE READING CHART – WEEK EIGHT							
Beginning Date:				Verses Total for **Week Eight**:			
Sunday	Monday	Tuesday	Wednesday	Thursday	Friday	Saturday	

BIBLE READING CHART	
Beginning Date: _____ Ending Date: _____	GRAND TOTAL_____

RAP = Read And Pray

Prayer requests record example:

(John 5:39 and Luke 24:45)
*"Lord, teach us to "Search the scriptures; for in them
we have eternal life: and they testify of You.
Then You will open our understanding,
that we might understand the scriptures."*

Date:	Request:	Answer:
Example:	*That I may glorify You today.	*I shared JESUS with my neighbor.
	*Have an opportunity to share Jesus.	
	*Save my friend/family _____	*My doctor had good news.
	*Health.	
	*Government leaders.	*My pastor preached a wonderful message.
	*Pastors.	
	Etc.	

Date:	Request:	Answer:

Date:	Request:	Answer:

(Bonus points = 500 page)

RAP = Read And Pray

Journal your chosen Scriptures below.
List book, chapter and verses:

_____
_____
_____
_____
_____
_____
_____
_____
_____
_____
_____

Write out your prayer for these Scriptures below:

_____
_____
_____
_____
_____
_____
_____
_____
_____
_____
_____
_____
_____
_____
_____

(Bonus points = 500 page)

RAP = Read And Pray

Study/Learning Charts

RAP = Read And Pray
(Memorize)

10 Commandments

1. Thou shalt have no other gods before me.
2. Thou shalt not make unto thee any graven image.
3. Thou shalt not take the name of the LORD thy God in vain.
4. Remember the sabbath day, to keep it holy.
5. Honor thy father and thy mother.
6. Thou shalt not kill.
7. Thou shalt not commit adultery.
8. Thou shalt not steal.
9. Thou shalt not bear false witness.
10. Thou shalt not covet.

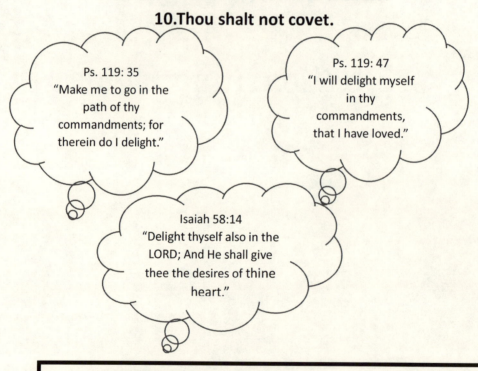

Ps. 119: 35
"Make me to go in the path of thy commandments; for therein do I delight."

Ps. 119: 47
"I will delight myself in thy commandments, that I have loved."

Isaiah 58:14
"Delight thyself also in the LORD; And He shall give thee the desires of thine heart."

> The first four commandments deal with
> God's holiness and our relationship with Him.
> The last six deal with our reasonable responsibilities
> to ourselves and mankind.

RAP = Read And Pray

Below list the Scriptures you can currently quote and/or
The Scriptures you plan to memorize:

RAP = Read And Pray

10 Commandments (Exodus 20)
Write Out - THE 10 COMMANDMENTS

1.
_____
_____

2.
_____
_____

3.
_____
_____

4.
_____
_____

5.
_____
_____

6.
_____
_____

7.
_____
_____

8.
_____
_____

9.
_____
_____

10.
_____
_____

(Bonus points = 500 page)

RAP = Read And Pray

Prayer Record

Date:	Requests:	Answer:

Date:	Requests:	Answer:

Date:	Requests:	Answer:

(Bonus points = 500 page)

"Lord, teach us to <u>search</u> the scriptures;
for in them we have eternal life:
and they testify of You.
Then You will open our understanding,
that we might understand the scriptures."
(John 5:39 and Luke 24:45)

RAP = Read And Pray

Memorizing the twelve disciples and learning important details about each will help you distinguish them and their roll in fulfilling prophecy and see the bigger picture of the mission for church as we see it today. Their lives are examples to us in how to live daily for Christ.

Memorize the 12 Disciples

Memory hint: Alphabetically: –A B J J J J M P P S T T
Write out the names below and use this tool to remember all of them.

Andrew
Bartholomew
James (Son of Alpheus)
James (Brother of John)
John
Judas Iscariot
Matthew
Peter
Philip
Simon
Thaddeus (also known as Jude)
Thomas

A_____

B_____

J_____

J_____

J--------

J_____

M_____

P_____

P_____

S_____

T_____

T_____

(Bonus points = 500 page)

RAP = Read And Pray

Write out facts about the 12 Disciples:

Andrew

_____
_____
_____
_____
_____
_____
_____

Bartholomew

_____
_____
_____
_____
_____

James (Son of Alpheus)

_____
_____
_____
_____
_____
_____

(Bonus points = 500 page)

RAP = Read And Pray

James (Brother of John)

_____
_____
_____
_____
_____
_____

John

_____
_____
_____
_____
_____
_____
_____
_____

Judas Iscariot

_____
_____
_____
_____
_____
_____

(Bonus points = 500 page)

RAP = Read And Pray

Matthew

_____
_____
_____
_____
_____
_____

Peter

_____
_____
_____
_____
_____
_____
_____
_____
_____

Philip

_____
_____
_____
_____
_____
_____

(Bonus points = 500 page)

RAP = Read And Pray

Simon

_____
_____
_____
_____
_____
_____
_____

Thaddeus (Jude)

_____
_____
_____
_____
_____
_____
_____

Thomas

_____
_____
_____
_____
_____
_____
_____

(Bonus points = 500 page)

RAP = Read And Pray

Prayer Requests Record

Date:	Requests:	Answer:

Date:	Requests:	Answer:

Date:	Requests:	Answer:

"Lord, teach us to <u>search</u> the scriptures;
for in them we have eternal life:
and they testify of You.
Then You will open our understanding,
that we might understand the scriptures."
(John 5:39 and Luke 24:45)

RAP = Read And Pray

Twelve sons of Jacob

Jacob's first 4 sons: Reuben, Simeon, Levi, Judah.
Circle that tribe became the priests for Israel?

Reuben
Simeon
Levi
Judah
Dan
Naphtali
Gad
Asher
Issachar
Zebulun
Joseph
Benjamin

Joseph's (Tribe) became two Tribes named after his sons. Name the two sons:

1.

2.

Draw a line to that tribe The Messiah descended?
Matthew 1:16

Why is Levi, the 3rd son of Jacob, not considered an inherited tribe?

Research the 12 Tribes of Israel:

According to Hebrew scriptures, the 12 tribes are the descendants of the Biblical patriarch Jacob, also known as Israel, and his wives and concubines. The tribes are named after ten of Jacob's sons: Reuben, Simeon, Judah, Dan, Naphtali, Gad, Asher, Issachar, Zebulun and Benjamin. The tribe of Levi became the chosen tribe of priests (giving up inheritance of the promised land) and the (tribe) of Joseph was given to his two sons: Ephraim and Manasseh. Making the 12 tribes of Israel as: Reuben, Simeon, Judah, Dan, Naphtali, Gad, Asher, Issachar, Zebulon, Ephraim, Manasseh, and Benjamin.

After the death of King Solomon in 922 BC, the 10 northern tribes established the independent Kingdom of Israel. The other two tribes, Judah and Benjamin formed the Kingdom of Judah.

(It's important not to skip this exercise because these twelve sons of Jacob as well as his grandchildren and other family members play a part in total understanding of the entire Bible which will be revealed to you in time as you study it in whole.)

(Bonus points = 500 page)

RAP = Read And Pray

Journal your chosen Scriptures below.
List book, chapter and verses:

_____
_____
_____
_____
_____
_____
_____
_____
_____
_____
_____

Write out your prayer for these Scriptures below:

_____
_____
_____
_____
_____
_____
_____
_____
_____
_____
_____
_____

(Bonus points = 500 page)

RAP = Read And Pray

On this page write out your research concerning
The tribe of Israel and The tribe of Judah:

(1000 bonus points)

RAP = Read And Pray

ABRAHAM – SARAH
ISAAC – REBEKAH
JACOB

List the names of the sons to their birth mothers.

LEAH	RACHEL	BILHAH (Rachel's Handmaid)	ZILPAH Leah's Handmaid)
1	11	5	7
2	12	6	8
3			
4			
9			
10			

Learn in order of their birth and birth mother.

1. Reuben
2. Simeon
3. Levi
4. Judah
5. Dan
6. Naphtali
7. Gad
8. Asher
9. Issachar
10. Zebulun
11. Joseph
12. Benjamin

(Bonus points = 500 page)

RAP = Read And Pray

Promise was given to Abraham

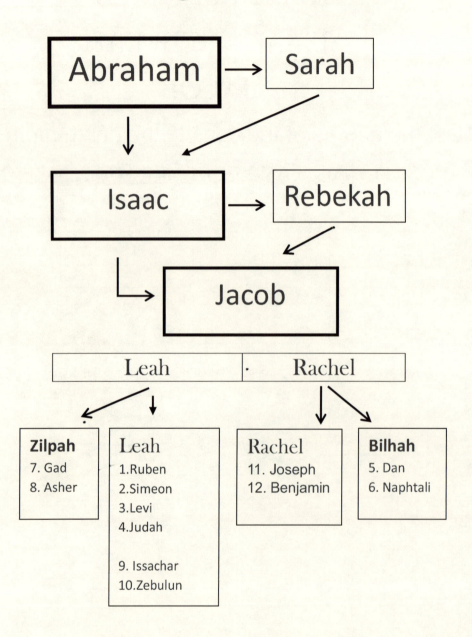

RAP = Read And Pray

Jacob's name was changed to Israel after he wrestled an angel of the Lord. The tribes are part of the Hebrew Bible and the traditional divisions of the ancient Jewish people. Below write out facts about each of the twelve sons (tribes) namesake.

<u>Reuben</u>: Means "look, a son!" or "the Lord has seen my affliction"

_____
_____
_____
_____
_____

<u>Simeon</u>: Means "man of hearing" or "the Lord has heard me"

_____
_____
_____
_____
_____

<u>Levi</u>: Means "joined" or "wrapped around like an embrace"

_____
_____
_____
_____

Why did Levi not receive an inheritance or be named as one of the 12 tribes?

_____
_____
_____
_____

(Bonus points = 500 page)

RAP = Read And Pray

<u>Judah</u>: Means "to praise out of a feeling of gratitude"

_____
_____
_____
_____
_____
_____
_____
_____

<u>Dan</u>: Means "judge"

_____
_____
_____
_____
_____
_____
_____
_____

<u>Naphtali</u>: Means "twisting"

_____
_____
_____
_____
_____
_____
_____
_____

(Bonus points = 500 page)

RAP = Read And Pray

Gad: Means "fortune"

_____
_____
_____
_____

Asher: Means "happy"

_____
_____
_____
_____

Issachar: Means "man of the higher"

_____
_____
_____
_____

Zebulun: Means "one who is exalted and honored"

_____
_____
_____
_____

(Bonus points = 500 page)

RAP = Read And Pray

<u>Joseph</u>: Means "fruitful bow" or "fruitful son"

_____
_____
_____
_____
_____
_____
_____
_____

Joseph's sons, <u>Ephraim & Manasseh</u>: Ephraim means "doubly fruitful" and Manasseh means "one who causes to forget pain" or "relieved from the condition of debt".

_____
_____
_____
_____
_____

<u>Benjamin</u>: Means "son of the right hand"

_____
_____
_____
_____
_____
_____
_____
_____
_____

(Bonus points = 500 page)

RAP = Read And Pray

Scriptures on Salvation

Easy as A B C

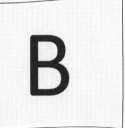
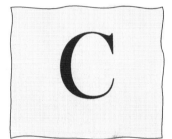

Admit: You are a _ _ _ _ _ _ .

Write out Roman 3:23

Believe God's P _ _ _ _ _ _ _ _ .

Write out John 3:16

(Bonus points = 500 page)

RAP = Read And Pray

Confess. sins and accept the gift of salvation.

Write out Roman 10:9-13

**Name five steps of the
PLAN OF SALVATION
(See page 77)**

1.
2.
3.
4.
5.

(Bonus points = 500 page)

RAP = Read And Pray

Journal your chosen Scriptures below.
List book, chapter and verses:

_____
_____
_____
_____
_____
_____
_____
_____
_____
_____
_____

Write out your prayer for these Scriptures below:

_____
_____
_____
_____
_____
_____
_____
_____
_____
_____
_____

(Bonus points = 500 page)

RAP = Read And Pray

Name the 7 men who lived to be over 900 years old.
List Scriptures where these are found.

1. _____
   _____
2. _____
   _____
3. _____
   _____
4. _____
   _____
5. _____
   _____
6. _____
   _____
7. _____
   _____

(Bonus points = 500 page)

Notes:

RAP = Read And Pray

Name the 10 plagues of Egypt & Scripture where found.

1. _____

2. _____

3. _____

4. _____

5. _____

6. _____

7. _____

8. _____

9. _____

10. _____

(Bonus points = 500 page)

RAP = Read And Pray

Name the Beatitudes: *Blessed are:*

1.

2.

3.

4.

5.

6.

7.

8.

9.

(Bonus points = 500 page)

RAP = Read And Pray

Answer and list Scripture reference:

1. Name the four Gospels.

2. How many chapters are in the entire Bible?

3. What is the shortest chapter?

4. What is the longest chapter?

5. In what unusual place did Peter find a coin to pay taxes?

6. What is the longest verse of the Bible?

7. What seasoning did Jesus say Christians' lives should be like?

8. What group of people did not believe in the resurrection of the dead: the Pharisees or the Sadducees?

9. Jesus compared faith to what seed?

10. What relationship was Jesus to John the Baptist?

11. Where is "apple of the eye" mentioned in the Bible?

12. Who was Dorcas?

(Bonus points = 500 page)

RAP = Read And Pray

LIFE VERSES

Choose and list four of your favorite verses & memorize.

1.

_____

2.

_____

3.

_____

4.

_____

(Bonus points = 500 page)

RAP = Read And Pray

List the books of the New Testament and each author.

	Book	Author
1.		
2.		
3.		
4.		
5.		
6.		
7.		
8.		
9.		
10.		
11.		
12.		
13.		
14..		
15.		
16.		
17.		
18.		
19.		
20.		
21.		
22.		
23.		
24.		
25.		
26.		
27.		

(Bonus points = 500 pages

RAP = Read And Pray

Name the seven statements of Jesus

Found in the book of John

	JESUS SAID: I AM:	
John 6:35		State why this is important to spiritual growth:
John 8:12		State why this is important to spiritual growth:
John 10:7,9		State why this is important to spiritual growth:
John 10:11,14		State why this is important to spiritual growth:
John 11:25		State why this is important to spiritual growth:
John 14:6		State why this is important to spiritual growth:
John 15:1,5		State why this is important to spiritual growth:

(Bonus points = 500 page)

RAP = Read And Pray

Journal your chosen Scriptures below.
List book, chapter and verses:

_____
_____
_____
_____
_____
_____
_____
_____
_____
_____
_____

Write out your prayer for these Scriptures below:

_____
_____
_____
_____
_____
_____
_____
_____
_____
_____
_____
_____

(Bonus points = 500 page)

RAP = Read And Pray

Extra bonus page for Chapter 1:

Has chapter 1 been a challenge to you? If so, how?

List some of the most important things you have learned in your study of chapter 1:

Has this study helped you learn to use your *Concordance* in the back of your Bible in order to locate Scripture verses?

Using your *Concordance* find the following two verses and document where it is found in the Bible.

> *"Have not I commanded thee? Be strong and of a good courage;
> be not afraid, neither be thou dismayed: for the LORD thy God
> is with thee whithersoever thou goest."*

Found in:_____

> *"But, beloved, be not ignorant of this one thing,
> that one day is with the Lord as a thousand years,
> and a thousand years as one day."*

Found in:_____

(Bonus points = 500 page)

RAP = Read And Pray

Chapter 2

Reading
The Bible

RAP = Read And Pray

*How we got the Bible
* The major divisions of the Bible
*Bible overview

RAP = Read And Pray

Benefit of Bible reading
The Bible *contains*

The secret of peace with God.

*"Rejoice in the Lord always: and again I say, Rejoice.
Let your moderation be known unto all men. The Lord is at hand.
Be careful for nothing; but in everything by prayer and supplication with thanksgiving let your requests be made known unto God,
And the peace of God, that passeth all understanding, shall keep your hearts and minds through Christ Jesus.
Finally, brethren, whatsoever things are true, whatsoever things are honest, whatsoever things are just, whatsoever things are pure, whatsoever things are lovely whatsoever things are of good report; if there be any virtue, and if there be any praise, think on these things."
Philippians 4:4-8*

RAP = Read And Pray

Benefit of Bible reading
The Bible *teaches*

<u>That Christian character is produced by
The Holy Spirit, not by self-effort.</u>

*"But the fruit of the Spirit is love, joy, peace,
long suffering, gentleness, goodness, faith,
Meekness, temperance: against such there is no law.
And they that are Christ's have crucified the flesh
with the affection and lusts.
If we live in the Spirit, let us also walk in the Spirit."
Galatians 5:22-25*

RAP = Read And Pray

Why is the Bible called *The Holy* Bible?

Key points

1. The Bible is inspired by God – this is the reason it is called "God's Holy Word".

   II Timothy 3:16-17 "All Scripture is given by inspiration of God, and is profitable for doctrine, for reproof, for correction, for instruction in righteousness: that the man of God may be perfect, thoroughly furnished unto all good works."
   2 Peter 1:20-21 "Knowing this first, that no prophecy of the scripture is of any private interpretation. For the prophecy came not in old time by the will of man: but holy men of God spake as they were moved by the Holy Ghost."

Every word in the Bible is true. If it came from God – there is no lie in it! Therefore, all scripture in the Bible can be taken literal and absolute. Deuteronomy 12:32 – *"What thing soever I command you, observe to do it: thou shalt not add thereto, nor diminish from it."*

Personal opinions do not qualify as scriptural.

2. The Bible is made up of 66 different books that were written over 1,600 years (from approximately 1500 BC to AD 100) by more than 40 kings, prophets, leaders, and followers of Jesus. The Old Testament has 39 books (written approximately 1500 – 400 BC). The New Testament has 27 books (written approximately 45-100 AD).

   Hebrews 4:12 "For the Word of God is quick, and powerful, and sharper than any two-edged sword, piercing even to the dividing asunder of soul and spirit, and of the joints and marrow, and is a discerner of the thoughts and intents of the heart."

The Bible is accurate with no errors. Anyone who sets out to prove it wrong will fail. The Old Testament prophecies were fulfilled in the New Testament as the Messiah came as promised. Jesus Christ is the Son of God and 100% God as well as 100% in a human body. The Bible is the Greatest of all books and His Word will live forever. It does what no other piece of literature can.

3. The books of the Bible were collected, arranged and recognized as inspired sacred authority by councils of rabbis and councils of church leaders based on careful guidelines. They were protected and read to eager listeners who also recognized the holiness of the Scripture, therefore, to please God they had to obey the Scriptures. Followers of God must reverence His Word in daily living and believe that the prophecy of the coming Messiah, was fulfilled in Jesus Christ.

RAP = Read And Pray

> *Luke 4:17-21 "And there was delivered unto him the book of the prophet Esaias. And when he had opened the book, He found the place where it was written. The Spirit of the Lord is upon me. Because he hath anointed me to preach the gospel to the poor; he hath sent me to heal the brokenhearted, to preach deliverance to the captives and recovering of sight to the blind, To set at liberty them that are bruised, To preach the acceptable year of the Lord. And he closed the book, and He gave it again to the minister, and sat down. And the eyes of all them that where in the synagogue were fastened on Him. And He began to say unto them, This day is this scripture fulfilled in your ears."*

<u>Jesus Christ is the fulfillment of all Scripture.</u>
<u>The Bible is recorded history and documented true events, testified by eyewitnesses.</u>

4. Before the printing press was invented, the Bible was copied by hand. The Bible was copied very accurately and in many cases by special scribes who developed intricate methods of counting words and letters to insure that no errors had been made. The Bible was the first book ever printed on the printing press with moveable type. (Gutenberg Press, 1455, Latin Bible).

5. There is much evidence that the Bible we have today is remarkably true to the original writings. The Dead Sea Scrolls confirmed the astonishing reliability of some of the copies of the Old Testament made over the years. Although some spelling variations exist, no variation affected basic Bible doctrines. By 200 AD, the Bible was translated into seven languages and currently some portions of the Bible have been translated in 3,658 different languages.

6. Note of awareness. Not all versions of the Bible contain the original meaning as inspired by God. Some say there have been over 900 translations into English alone. It's no wonder that people get confused as to that is what and what is that. If you fall into this category, please pray for guidance as to that version is meant for you to understand and still be true to the original meaning as inspired by God. As is true – "not every church follows the Gospel, nor does every preacher preach it." *This is why personal Bible study is so important to spiritual growth.* Check it out for yourself and be sure that what you are being told coincides with God's true intention. Just because something is believed, does not make it true. So be sure you believe it <u>*because it is true;*</u> not just make it true to you because you believe it. In other words ask yourself: "Is it true because I believe it; or do I believe it because it is true"?

RAP = Read And Pray

The Major Divisions of the Bible

There are five major divisions of the Old Testament: 1.– The Pentateuch. 2. – The books of History. 3. – The books of Poetry & Wisdom. 4. – The Major Prophets. 5. – The Minor Prophets.

<u>The Pentateuch</u> is composed of the first five books of the Old Testament Hebrew Bible that is traditionally ascribed to Moses. It is now held by scholars to be a compilation from texts of the 9th to 5th centuries BC. The word itself simply means *five books*. These five books are also called – 'The Books of Law'. They are Genesis, Exodus, Leviticus, Numbers, and Deuteronomy. Genesis means *the beginning*. Exodus simply means *to exit*. Leviticus is the term coming from the tribe of Levi, who were the priest. Numbers means *numbers*. And Deuteronomy means *second law* or *repeated law*.

The Book of **Genesis** speaks of truth of Creation and all things in the beginning. It means *origin creation* and *start*. We need not look anywhere else for proof of a higher power, for there is none other than God Almighty.

The Book of **Exodus** happened with the mass departure of the Israelites from Egypt. The Passover festival celebrates this Exodus. The mighty works of plaques are listed therein, as well as mighty miracles of deliverance. The 10 Commandment issued to Moses on the Mount, are recorded in Exodus 20.

The **Levitical Law** deals with laws and sacrifices. We are most blessed to live under grace than to try to fulfill all the requirements held in the book of Leviticus.

The Book of **Numbers** recounts the results of the disobedience of the Israelites, and the results of not having faith in God. Specifically, it focuses on the Israelites' failure to uphold their commitment to God and the subsequent punishment of being kept out of the Promised Land. It is the sacred history of the Israelites as they wandered in the wilderness. The book is a reminder that God remains true to His covenantal purpose despite Israel's repeated failure.

The Book of **Deuteronomy** is about obeying God and is the final address to second-generation Israel. Its purpose is to challenge and exhort this generation to total devotion to the Lord within a renewed covenant relationship and promising blessings for loyalty and at the same time threatening curses for rebellion.

Without a study of these books, one cannot fully appreciate what it means to be saved by grace and redeemed by the blood of the perfect lamb sacrifice of Jesus Christ.

RAP = Read And Pray

BIBLE OVERVIEW

Old Testament - 39 Books

PENTATEUCH (books of Moses)	HISTORICAL (books of Law)	POETRY/WISDOM	MINOR PROPHETS
Genesis	Joshua	Job	Hosea
Exodus	Judges	Psalms	Joel
Leviticus	Ruth	Proverbs	Amos
Numbers	1 Samuel	Ecclesiastes	Obadiah
Deuteronomy	2 Samuel	Song of Solomon	Jonah
	1 Kings		Micah
Pentateuch Simply means *five books* (that the Jews call the Torah)	2 Kings	**MAJOR PROPHETS**	Nahum
	1 Chronicles	Isaiah	Habakkuk
	2 Chronicles	Jeremiah	Zephaniah
	Ezra	Lamentations	Haggai
	Nehemiah	Ezekiel	Zechariah
	Esther	Daniel	Malachi

New Testament - 27 Books

Gospels & Acts	Paul's Epistles (Letters)		General Epistles & Revelation
Matthew	Romans	1 Thessalonians	Hebrew
Mark	1 Corinthians	2 Thessalonians	James
Luke	2 Corinthians	1 Timothy	1 Peter
John	Galatians	2 Timothy	2 Peter
Acts	Ephesians	Titus	1 John
	Philippians	Philemon	2 John
	Colossians		3 John
Luke wrote two of these books. Luke & Acts The other three authored the book bearing his name.	Some scholars consider Paul wrote the Book of Hebrews also in addition to these 13 books. James, Peter, and Jude authored the books bearing their names.		Jude
			Revelation
			Gospel of **John**, 1st, 2nd, 3rd **John** and **Revelation** were written by John

RAP = Read And Pray

Old Testament Synopsis

GENESIS "The Beginning" Creation, fall, flood, Abraham, Isaac, Jacob, Joseph. Demonstrates that God is sovereign and loves His creation.
EXODUS Moses, The Plagues & The Exodus. It shows God's faithfulness to the covenant and provides Israel with guidelines for holy living. The Ten Commandments.
LEVITICUS Laws, sacrifices, Priesthood, clean/unclean, Day of Atonement.
NUMBERS Census, History, Exhibits what happens when people rebel against God.
DEUTERONOMY Sermons of Moses, journey, laws, covenant and farewell.
JOSHUA History of conquest. To assure people that obedience to God is rewarded.
JUDGES To stress the importance of remaining loyal to God. Including the Judges; Deborah, Gideon, and Samson.
RUTH Story of Ruth, a faithful foreigner. Demonstrates loyalty and love for God.
1 Samuel History of events concerning Samuel, Saul and David.
2 Samuel History of David's reign, victories, sin with Bathsheba. Family problems and forgiveness, prominence of David's lineage and conclusions.
1 KINGS Covers King Solomon's reign, Temple construction, Queen of Sheba, Kingdom splits, and Prophet Elijah. The value of obeying and the danger of disobeying.
2 KINGS In exile in Babylon. The Prophet Elisha, Kings of Judah and Israel, Fall of Israel, King Josiah, Fall of Judah.
1 CHRONICLES Review of David's reign, To encourage the remnant.
2 CHRONICLES Highlights of Kings of Judah, To show the benefits of obedience.
EZRA History of Reconstruction, The exiles return, rebuilding the Temple, Ezra's works.
NEHEMIAH Rebuilding of the walls of Jerusalem. Threats, persecution, renewal of covenant, dedication and laws.
ESTHER Story of Redemption. Search for new Queen, Haman's plot, Esther's plan to pray, Haman's downfall and Esther saves the Jews.
JOB Story of Job's perseverance. To show sovereignty of God in suffering. Job tested, Job's friends, Elihu's speech, God's answer.
PSALMS Poetry and Song. To communicate with God and worship Him.
PROVERBS Provide wisdom and guidance for God's children, Wise sayings, Solomon's words, other Proverbs.
ECCLESIASTES A Search to discover truth. Life is not always fair, No one knows the future, obedience to God.
SONG of SOLOMON Love poem. The courtship, The wedding, The lasting relationship.
ISAIAH Prophecy and judgment. Convince people that salvation comes through repentance and hope in the coming Messiah. Future hope.
JEREMIAH Warn Judah of their destruction, remind them of their sin, New Covenant, and Fall of Jerusalem.
LAMENTATIONS Express the despair of the people of Judah over the loss of their land, city, and temple. Hope and mercy, punishment, and restoration.
EZEKIEL Prophecy and warning. To confront people about their sin, Give them one last chance to repent and offer hope.
DANIEL Daniel and his friends, The lion's den, apocalyptic visions. (Destruction of the World). Future redemption. A Kingdom that will never be destroyed.

RAP = Read And Pray

> **HOSEA, JOEL, AMOS, OBADIAH, JONAH, MICAH, NAHUM, HABAKKUK, ZEPHANIAH, HAGGAI, ZECHARIAH, MALACHI**
>
> The 12 Minor Prophets, called "The Book of the Twelve" in The Hebrew Bible, are just as important as the Major Prophets. They are called 'minor' because of the short length of the books. They also brought God's Word to the people regarding judgment and hope. Includes: The unfaithful wife, blessings and curses, Israel's destruction, Israel's victory. Shows God loves all people, restoration, mercy, God in control, tough questions, praise, promises, motivation, priority for God, and Godly love.

New Testament Synopsis

The New Testament begins with the Four Gospels. In your search for events, teachings, and explanations for truth of Jesus Christ being the one and only Son of God and the true way to heaven, you must search these books in the New Testament for proof and eyewitness testimonies of times when Jesus walked the earth in man-form and as 100% God. It is vitally important to listen to Jesus' own words when forming an opinion concerning the truth of the entirety of the Holy Bible, The Word of God. That is the basis for all hope of salvation. The Gospels contain the same stories in part or whole, as a way of soothing the human mind that there is more than one proof of the truth that Jesus Christ is "The Messiah." He was born of a virgin, lived, walked the earth, died, was buried, and was risen from the death, reappearing in human form. He then ascended to heaven with the promise of returning.

There are absolutely no flaws in these truths. No, not one. Testimonies confirmed it and history records it as facts.

Acts (written by Luke) is also included with the Gospels of Matthew, Mark, Luke, and John as eyewitnesses of the resurrection of Jesus Christ. It vividly and beautifully tells the story of Paul the Apostle and his untimely encounter with Jesus on the road to Damascus. Saul was chosen to be an evangelist/missionary who would preach the Gospel to the gentiles. He was renamed by Jesus to be called 'Paul'. Paul became the writer of a great number of the other books of the New Testament. He received this calling by the person Jesus Christ – *Himself*. This encounter was told first by a person other than Paul who could verify the truth of the events of Paul's claim to have met Jesus on the road to Damascus. Paul's life changed from a persecutor of Christians to become a believer who would be instrumental in the shaping the new Church age through his inspired epistles.

RAP = Read And Pray

The Gospels & Acts

MATTHEW - Written AD 60 by Matthew (the tax collector) in Judea. Records Jesus' birth and early life, ministry of Christ and His death and resurrection. Shows Jesus' lineage to David, the Kingly Messiah who fulfills prophecy.

MARK - Written AD 50s by John Mark in Rome. Records the ministry of Christ and His death and resurrection. It also shows Jesus as the suffering Son of Man who was sent to serve and not be served. John Mark would later be one of Paul's traveling companions on mission.

LUKE – Written by Luke (the physician) AD 60-62 in Caesarea. Records the birth, early life and ministry of Christ, as well as His death and resurrection. It shows Jesus as the Savior of the world who has compassion for all human beings.

JOHN – Written by John (the beloved disciple) AD 85 – 95 in Asia Minor. Records an introduction, public and private ministry of Christ and His death and resurrection. John shows Jesus as the Son of God, the Word made flesh, and Who provides eternal life for all who believe in Him. John also wrote 1st, 2nd, 3rd John and the book of Revelation (prophecy of end times). Jesus trusted John with this information and vision, I feel, because of their close friendship as well as respect for Jesus' Lordship.

ACTS – Also Written by Luke, AD 60-62 in Caesarea and Rome. Records the radical change and acts of the followers of Jesus after His resurrection and ascension. Introduction of the Holy Spirit in new believers and the missionary journeys of Paul as well as the spread of the gospel to the Jews and Gentiles.

Notes:

RAP = Read And Pray

The Gospels & Act
Select key verses from the books below
and write them in the spaces provided.

MATTHEW -
MARK –
LUKE –
JOHN –
ACTS –

(Bonus points = 500 page)

RAP = Read And Pray

The Apostle Paul wrote 13 books (letters) to churches, pastors and friends in order to guide, encourage, and correct them
ROMANS – Written to Roman Christians, AD 57 to illustrate law, faith, and holy living. The Romans Road to Salvation.
1 CORINTHIANS – Letter to Church in Corinth, AD 55-56. Addresses division and immorality, plus spiritual gifts and resurrection.
2 CORINTHIANS – Written from Philippi, AD 56 to the Church in Corinth. Speaks of Apostle characteristics, authority. Topic of giving.
GALATIANS – Letter to Church in Galatia from Asia Minor, AD 48-49 or 54-55. Warns against legalism, defends justification by faith.
EPHESIANS – Letter to Church in Ephesus while Paul was in prison in Rome, AD 60-62. Spiritual blessings even in difficult times.
PHILIPPIANS – Letter to Church in Philippi also while Paul was in prison in Rome, AD 60-62. Paul expresses his love for the Philippines, joys of life, humility of Christ, finishing the race.
COLOSSIANS – Letter to Church in Colossae also while Paul was in prison in Rome, AD 60-62. Teaches authority of Christ as head over every power. (2:9-10). Thanksgiving and faithfulness to the end.
1 THESSALONIANS – Letter to Church in Thessalonica, AD 50-52. faith and example. living daily for God. Christ's return, joy, continual praying.
2 THESSALONIANS – Letter to Church in Thessalonica, AD 50-52. emphasizes Christ return, prayer, work, obedience to God, perseverance.
1 TIMOTHY - Written to Timothy, AD 62-66. Concern for the Church in Ephesus. Church leadership, false teachers, discipline, advice.
2 TIMOTHY – Second letter to Timothy while Paul was in prison in Rome, AD 66-67. Encourage Timothy to stay faithful in ministry even in the midst of suffering. Authority of God's Word, living a Godly life.
TITUS – Letter to Titus, AD 64-66. Rome. To encourage the Church in Crete to do good works. Instruction for Titus, living by faith and final instructions.
PHILEMON – Letter to Philemon while in prison in Rome, AD 60-62. Different from other letters as Paul instructs Philemon to forgive and receive Onesimus, a runaway slave. Philemon's love and faith.

RAP = Read And Pray

Select one key verse from the books below and write it in the space provided.
ROMANS –
1 CORINTHIANS –
2 CORINTHIANS –
GALATIANS –
EPHESIANS –
PHILIPPIANS –
COLOSSIANS –
1 THESSALONIANS –
2 THESSALONIANS – .
1 TIMOTHY - -
2 TIMOTHY –
TITUS –
PHILEMON –

(Bonus points = 500 page)

RAP = Read And Pray

General Epistles (messages) & Revelation

HEBREWS – Paul or Unknown, AD 60-69. Letter to Hebrews believers. Emphasizes the New Covenant of Christ Jesus over the Old Covenant. Supremacy of Christ, New Covenant, Life of Faith.

JAMES – Written by James, (Half-brother of Jesus, that is another proof that Jesus is the Messiah – James speaks of Him as (LORD) even though he grew up with Jesus.) AD 49 from Jerusalem to the Jewish believers. Faith, works, speech, and wisdom.
James 1:1 "James, a servant of God and of the Lord Jesus Christ, to the Twelve Tribes that are scattered abroad, greetings."

1 PETER – Written by Peter as open letter to all Christians, AD 64-65 from Rome. Covers holiness, submission, suffering, and advice to the old and the young.

2 PETER – Written by Peter as before. Contains warnings against false teachers, living like Christ, and the return of Christ.

1 JOHN – Written by John (beloved disciple) AD 85-95 from Ephesus. Emphasized love in Christ, To do so means to: *Live in the Light - Live in Love - - Live by Faith.*

2 JOHN – As these other two books in place and time. Warns against sacrilege, disrespect, blaspheme and false teachers.

3 JOHN – As these other two books in place and time but especially written to Gaius.
3 John 4 - "I have no greater joy than to hear that my children walk in truth."

JUDE – Written by Jude between 60 – 80 AD. Scholars say Jude was a brother of James the Just and possibly a half-brother of Jesus. Very short book that warns of heresy. He understood troublesome times were coming but also gives assurance of the hope that is found in Jesus Christ.
v. 4. *"He (Jesus Christ) is able to keep you from falling and to present you before His glorious presence without fault and with great joy."*

REVELATION - Note: Revelation is 'one' combined to reveal a total revelation. It is not Revelation(s). The 5th book written by John the beloved, AD 90-96, from the Island of Patmos. The only book of prophecy in the New Testament. Yet to be fulfilled. Written to seven represented churches and holds deep visions from God covering God's triumph and the new creation. It encourages believers who are experiencing persecution and illustrates that God is in control at all times. The whole purpose of creation is to love and worship God. Therefore the goal of living is to develop fellowship with the creator.

RAP = Read And Pray

Select key verses from the books below and write it in the space provided.	
HEBREWS –.	
JAMES –	
1 PETER –	
2 PETER -	
1 JOHN –	
2 JOHN –	
3 JOHN –	
JUDE –	
REVELATION –	

(Bonus points = 500 page)

RAP = Read And Pray

Journal your chosen Scriptures below.
List book, chapter and verses:

_____
_____
_____
_____
_____
_____
_____
_____
_____
_____
_____
_____

Write out your prayer for these Scriptures below:

_____
_____
_____
_____
_____
_____
_____
_____
_____
_____
_____
_____
_____
_____

(Bonus points = 500 page)

RAP = Read And Pray

What have you learned from Chapter 2 concerning studying the Bible?

(Bonus points = 500 page)

RAP = Read And Pray

Chapter 3
Understanding Salvation

RAP = Read And Pray

The Worth of a Soul

Understanding the need for salvation is impossible to a self-justified person who believes they have no need to justify their actions. In other words – they are not lost and therefore have no need to be found. The first truth for such a person to understand is sin leaves a mark on the Soul inside the body and that mark must be erased before it is returned to God who gave it. *Your soul* is the most important part of your being. It came from God when He created you in your mother's womb and it will be returned to God when your body dies. At that point God knows if the soul will be united with a new body for heaven or a new body for hell. Either way, this new body God gives as a home for your soul is eternal, unlike our earthly fleshly body. The soul finds it final place to dwell for all eternity.

This is a truth that must be received by faith in God – The Creator of all things and people. Let me explain it this way. When you were created by God in the womb (Jeremiah 1:5) He gave you a living soul. The body grew around the soul. It is housed in the body until your death at that time it must return to God from where it came for final judgment of your soul's eternal existence. God will judge that based on your earthly decision of whether or not to receive forgiveness of sin through the birth, death and resurrection of His Son, Jesus Christ as payment for your sins. This fact puts your soul in a category all by itself. It is the most valuable thing you will ever have in this life and in the life to come.

A person has nothing to do with how they come into this world in their first body. No one, including you, gave instructions to your mother or father about what you wanted to look like when you were born. It was up to someone else. You had no choice in the matter. The body itself is not the most important part of your being; your soul is. How do I know for a certainty that your soul is created to live forever and the body you live in today is <u>not</u> created to live forever? It's simple, the Bible says so. As you have read the first part of Genesis in the Bible you read that "And the LORD God formed man of the dust of the ground and breathed into his nostrils the breath of life; and man <u>*became a living soul*</u>." (Genesis 2:7).

This Scripture does not say that man became a living body, it says man became a living *soul* and how did he become a living soul? Because God breathed into his nostrils *the breath of life*. Attached to this event is the true fact that God has always been and always will be. So in light of the fact that God shared one breathe with mankind, His one breath he breathed cannot die either. That gives *the soul* inside our body the right to live forever.

Stay with me, here is where things change. From the point of capability in decision making and knowing right from wrong, the soul has the freedom to choose for itself where it will live forever in its new body. This new body that God will design and ordain will have the same features of recognition but new feature of permanency. You consciously did not select the color of your skin or eyes or even when to be born; but your Soul definitely has a God given right to choose where it will spend eternity in its new body that will live forever.

Let me issue a warning here. If this appears far-fetched to you, then quit reading this and pick up a Bible. Understanding comes from the Scripture and eyes opened by the Holy Spirit. I cannot explain it; except by faith in the Holy Spirit's revelation. Every person's soul

RAP = Read And Pray

lives forever no matter what happens to their fleshly body. The body house of the soul that is saved by grace dies and decays into no useful thing; however, that sets the soul free to exit without the sting of death. Death holds no sting, and the grave holds no victory for the redeemed saved by grace. Sin is what makes death sting.

> *O death, where is thy sting? O grave, where is thy victory?*
> *The sting of death is sin; and the strength of sin is the law.*
> *But thanks be to God, that giveth us the victory through our Lord Jesus Christ.*
> *1 Corinthians 15:55-57*

For the Christian who has been redeemed by the blood of Jesus Christ this is God's promise therefore death is not a threat to our soul. Our existence contains the Body, the Soul, and the Spirit. The body will decay but not the soul. The soul chooses if it will be possessed by the Holy Spirit for eternal life or if it will refuse the Holy Spirit to keep self-will and condemnation. Therefore our life is in the soul – not the body and not the spirit. If it is well with your soul then your body does not fear death and your spirit is in a Holy state of being.

Oh that all the people in the entire world could understand the value of every person's soul. There is no price upon it for it is of great value that no one can afford or purchase. No one can steal it, destroy it, hide it or find it. It is the core of being and only the owner can surrender it.

When God placed your never-dying soul into your mother's womb, it was pure and holy. unscarred and unstained. We came from God innocent and holy and if we want to enter heaven, we must go back to God innocent and sanctified.

Friend, this is why the Cross was necessary. And this is why resurrection is reality. There are only two choices, heaven or hell. The choice is very simple. Choose Jesus, choose life. Rejecting Jesus is to reject God and heaven.

....

What is the worth of your soul?

What has left its stain on your soul?

What sin is worth eternal punishment?

Who offers eternal security for your soul? How?

RAP = Read And Pray

HAVING PEACE WITH GOD THROUGH
THE PLAN OF SALVATION

1 - Lost:
You are a sinner, lost with no hope to live in Heaven. Romans 3:10,23
"v.10.- "As it is written, There is none righteous, no, not one. v.23. For all have sinned and come short of the glory of God".

2 - Cost:
The wages of sin is death and hell. Romans 6:23
"For the wages of sin is death; but the gift of God is eternal life through Jeus Christ our Lord."

3 - Option:
You do not have to go to hell. The gift of Heaven is Free:
Ephesians 2:8-9 "For by grace are you saved through faith; and that not of yourselves: it is the ***gift*** of God."
Romans 5:8-9 "But God commendeth His love toward us in that, while we were yet sinners. Christ died for us. Much more then, being now justified by His blood, we shall be saved from wrath through Him.'

4 - How?
Confess, Believe.
John 1:12 "But as many as received Him. To them gave He power to become the sons of God, even to them that believe on His name."
John 3:16 "For God so loved the world that He gave His only begotten Son that whosoever believes on Him should not perish but have everlasting life".
John 3:18 "He that believeth on Him is not condemned: but he that believeth not is condemned already, because he hath not believed in the name of the only begotten Son of God."
Romans 10:9-13 "
That if thou shalt confess with thy mouth the Lord Jesus and shall believe in thine heart that God hath raised Him from the dead, thou shalt be saved. For with the heart man believeth unto righteousness; and with the mouth confession is made unto salvation. For the scripture saith, Whosoever believeth on Him shall not be ashamed. For there is no difference between the Jew and the Greek: for the same Lord over all is rich unto all that call upon Him. For whosoever shall call upon the name of the Lord ***shall be saved***."

5 - Pray & Claim – (Pray as led by the Holy Spirit) Sample:
Lord God, Heavenly Father, I confess you to be the Creator of all things and Jesus Christ is your one and only Son who came to this world as a sacrifice for my sins. He died on the Cross of Calvary and was raised from the dead. I ask your forgiveness for all my sins and ask you to give me the power to forgive those who have sinned against me. I repent and turn from my sins. I claim victory in Jesus. Fill me with your Holy Spirit. Thank you for saving me!
In the name of Jesus Christ, and for His sake, I pray. Amen.

RAP = Read And Pray

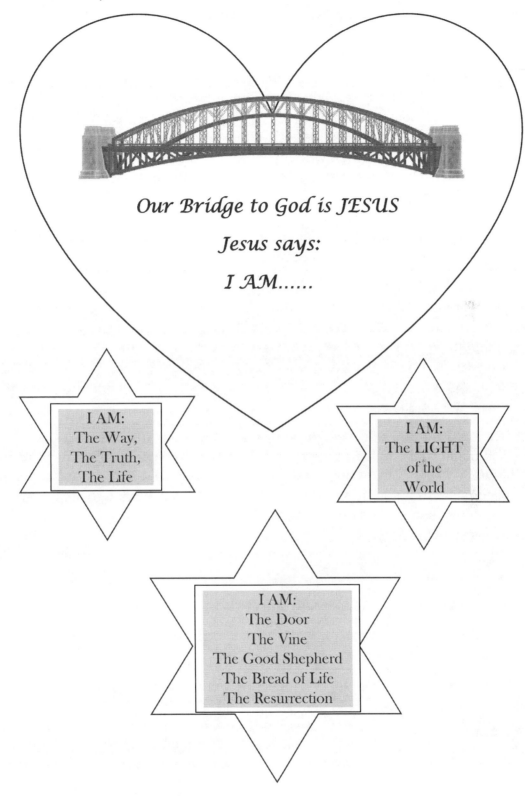

RAP = Read And Pray

Urgency of Salvation

Has your world ever been quaked? Has your soul ever trembled?

I remember the 1989 San Francisco earthquake when the freeway collapsed. Even though I was over 2,000 miles away, the event shook me and my world. Rescuers waited to recover bodies from cars crushed beneath the rubble hoping to find just one that could be rescued. The images that flooded the tv at that time were heart breaking. I felt for those trapped who might still be alive, knowing the situation was hopeless for them to receive immediate help. Over the years I've had a recurring dream that I needed help, but I could not scream for whatever reason. When I tried to scream only a weak squeak would come out. Perhaps the weak or silent screams of the lost needing deliverance are not heard by God's people. We walk pass such people every day in society. They know not what they need.

Christians are totally reliant on the Holy Spirit for guidance every single day of our lives. Why? Because we still live in a sin infested world. The self-centered "I" gets in our way. It is when "He" who is within me leads and guides every step that good things happen. People cannot always rely on a paper, script or internet connection to seek advice from God's Word. Paper burns and internet can shut down without warning. However Scripture embedded in a person's soul is secure at all times and readily available when prompted by the Holy Spirit.

I met Mary one Sunday and neither of us knew she would die the next day. Mary was a self-confessed drug addict desperate for hope, who came into our church that Sunday morning because of an invitation she received from a stranger standing in line behind her at the grocery store. This stranger had smiled and took the initiative to spark a conversation with Mary, sharing her name and where she went to church. As the days went by Mary never forgot that small act of kindness. The Sunday she came into our church looking for her two-minute friend she found more than just this friend, she found Jesus.

During prayer time before the morning message Mary stood up and said:

"My name is Mary; I am an addict. I don't want to be an addict, and something told me to go to church this morning."

When we left home that morning my husband did not know that the message he had been preparing all week was going to change. Coming down from the pulpit he asked Mary if she wanted to come up so the church could surround her with prayer, she nodded and immediate walked the aisle. As a few prayer warriors gathered around she began voluntarily telling her story and something wonderful happened that morning as the Holy Spirit began opening her eyes when our pastor started telling her Jesus' story. She had questions that he answered, and it was as natural as if they sat in the church office without other eyes watching. She was focused and totally in the moment and the unplanned bonus was our entire church got a lesson that morning about how to share the story of salvation by seeing it unfold. This could not have been scripted. It was an act of God.

Mary wanted to be baptized soon and she said she couldn't wait to tell others about what happened to her this morning. So that afternoon she began telling of her salvation experience only to be met by her boyfriend's anger that resulted in a beating so severe that she died the next day. She lived on earth as a Christian approximately twenty-four hours.

She never had the opportunity to learn the entire story of God the Father, Jesus the Son, the process of sanctification with the indwelling Holy Spirit, be baptized or join a church family. However, she went from condemned, to redeemed and justified, to glorified, all in the space of one short day.

Who can put a value on following the Holy Spirit when he urges a smile and a conversation while waiting in line somewhere? Who can put a value on following the Holy Spirit when he changes a sermon for looking into the eyes of a peace-seeking-person and seeing an opportunity to share the simple gospel of salvation? Who knows what impact seeing all this unfold has on the bench-sitter's desire to "go ye?"

The place and time of salvation is between God and the individual. God never saves anyone without them knowing it. Nor does He hide salvation from the seeker's heart. Judgment and confirmation of salvation belongs to God and only God. It does not belong to a particular denomination, church, preacher, family member, beloved neighbor or even a dreaded enemy. Confirmation of salvation is also not found in completion of any study course, confession to a priest behind a curtain, baptismal certification, church membership, donations, or personal sacrifice.

Salvation is so easy it's hard to believe. Yet, it is such a mystery that it baffles intellect. Salvation comes by faith in God's Word and produces a. *know-so* peace with God. No preacher can preach a man, women, boy or girl into heaven. Upon belief and faith in His Son, Jesus Christ, God gives redemption causing a person to be justified and once justified God begins immediately doing His work of sanctifying the believer for the ultimate glorification of the saved by grace. For the person who does not possess this know-so salvation there is an urgency to do so because the time is now. There is no guarantee of tomorrow and no one knows when Jesus will

RAP = Read And Pray

come to rapture the current believers who are ready to meet Him in the air. Being left behind when this happens will be a horrible inexplicable time on earth.

There is nothing that can be more important at this very second than to know that you know all is well with your soul.

That bridge is your soul on? #1_____ or #2_____

#1

#2

Write a thanksgiving prayer below to describe coming
from Picture #1 to safety in Picture #2:

_____

_____

(I claim no credit for the above photo or image.)

RAP = Read And Pray

"I AM" - Statements of Jesus

Jesus' "I AM" statements confirm Jesus knew exactly who He was. John 10:30 says that *"I and my Father are one."* John 14:11 - *"Believe me that I AM in the Father and the Father in me: or else believe me for the very works sake."*

Jesus is the One and Only perfect offering for our redemption.

Statement	Reference	When/Meaning/Warning	Promise
I AM… "The Bread of Life"	John 6:35	After Jesus fed the 5,000 people.	Bread sustains physical life, so Christ offers spiritual life that satisfies permanently, forever.
I AM… "The Light of the World"	John 8:12	This light shines from within a person who has been redeemed.	In a dark world where people stumble, Jesus offers Himself as a constant guide. Light is also symbolic of holiness.
I AM… "The door"	John 10:7,9	This door symbolizes an open heart to receive Jesus as our salvation.	Jesus is our security. By Him we can come into the presence of God Almighty. As the door, He is the only entrance to peace with God.
I AM… "The Good Shepherd"	John 10:11,14	Sheep are not very smart and can get themselves in much danger without a shepherd to look out for them, constantly.	Jesus is committed to always care for and keep watch over His people, just as a Shepherd would take care of his sheep. If one goes missing (MIA) -the Shepherd goes looking for him to bring him back to the flock.
I AM… "The Resurrection"	John 11:25	Jesus has the power to resurrect those who are stone dead in heart and soul; as well as physically, when He brought Lazarus back to life after he had been dead for 4 days.	Jesus as Lord has power to raise the dead and give them a new birth. (Born Again), with a new start. Death is not the final word. The soul lives forever, either in heaven or hell. He offers spiritually dead people the gift of eternal life.
I AM… "The Way" "The Truth" "The Life""	John 14:6	Jesus stated very simply that not only is He the way to heaven but also in Him there is always truth and life.	Jesus is the fulfillment of God's plan. The one and only way to the Father is by the Son. He offers spiritually dead people a new life by being born again.
I AM… The Vine	John 15:1,5	Jesus spoke this in the upper room on the night of his arrest.	By being attached to this vine, He enables eternal life to glow in and through the believer.

RAP = Read And Pray

Jesus Hours on the Cross

It is more than just 9:00 A.M. in Jerusalem.
It's Redemption Day

EVENTS BEFORE:
The Last Supper - Gethsemane - The Arrest - At the house of Caiaphas
Luke 22, Matthew 26 & John 18

<u>6:00AM</u> – Jesus before Pilate & Herod. Mark15:1, Luke 23:6-10
<u>8:00AM</u> – Returned to Pilate/Sentenced to die. Luke 23:11-24
<u>8:30AM</u> – Led to Calvary. Luke 23:26
<u>9:00AM</u> – THE CRUCIFIXION. Luke 23:33, Mark15:25
<u>9:00-11:00AM</u> - He was mocked/tortured. Matthew 27, Mark 15, Luke 23
<u>11:00-12:00</u> – One of the men who was being crucified with Jesus asked Jesus to save himself (and them) while the other criminal rebuked the idea and asked Jesus to be remembered when Jesus came into His Kingdom. Jesus said: *"today,* you will be with me in paradise." Luke 23:43
<u>NOON</u> – Darkness came over the whole land until the ninth hour. Mark 15:33 (12:00 – 3:00 PM)
<u>3:00PM</u> – Jesus's earthly body died. John 19:33-34, Revelation 1:18
(*Also see pages 194-195)

EVENTS IMMEDIATELY FOLLOWING:
The thieves' legs broken/The soldiers pierce Jesus' side. John:19:34
Earthquake/tombs break open/Centurion exclaimed "Surely, He was the Son of God! Matthew 27:54
The burial! John 19:38-42
The tomb is sealed. Matthew 27:66
(Mark's Gospel states actual times – "3rd hour, 6th hour, and 9th hour")
The day is done – but the best is coming! His Resurrection.

RAP = Read And Pray

Who is Jesus to you?

Just suppose you were hanging over a cliff clinging to a rope in hand, and you had no strength to climb up by yourself – who would you want to be holding the other end of that rope? Perhaps it might be: (A) a friend, (B) a neighbor, or (C) a beloved spouse?

When I answered this question, I thought of my husband because I knew he would hang onto that rope until all flesh was stripped off his hands and no energy left in his body. Do you have such a person in your life? If you have Jesus then you have someone better than a friend, neighbor, and even a beloved spouse. Jesus not only saves us from torment after this life is done but He also has power to "keep" us while we are on earth.

When we are weak, He is strong. He would also have the rope anchored and wrapped around the solid rock. A friend can't save you; a neighbor cannot save you, but Jesus (as your beloved) can. He is the rope, He is not only your best friend who will never leave you or forsake you – He is your way to the Father, and you are betrothed to Him – The King of Kings, and the Lord of Lords.

Jesus is:
our rope holder,
our friend,
our ever-present good neighbor,
our rope,
our anchor,
our rock -and,
He is most importantly our Savior.

No one goes through life without squabbles, disagreements, and misunderstandings that cause a breach in friendships or relationships all the way to the point of separations and/or to the point of parting paths permanently. Not so with Jesus. Reaching the end of the rope is not all bad because then may be the only time someone is willing to surrender. Too often people see no need for a higher power until they find themselves hopelessly in over their heads. In other words; totally broken, knowing they must have someone other than themselves to save them. It is at this point that eyes are open to see the way maker.

I knew a man who was having trouble "being saved". He had others praying for him (that is a very good thing) – but that was not enough. He also prayed himself and went to the altar at church for the pastor to pray with him. One day I was listening to him praying and I noticed that He was forgetting something. Even though he was asking God to help him find the way to peace, he was not admitting that he was lost and needed to be found. Since he was a very good family man he was missing the point that all our righteousness is as filthy rags in God's eyes and this needs to be confessed in order to see oneself in light of God's Holiness. During counseling this man saw himself as
a sinner who needed to be forgiven and he went on to spent the rest of his life serving Jesus as a child of the King.

RAP = Read And Pray

> *Isaiah 64:6*
> *"But we are all as an unclean thing,*
> *and all our righteousness are as filthy rags;*
> *and we all do fade as a leaf, and our iniquities,*
> *like the wind, have taken us away".*

People need a reason to seek God. People who think there is no personal responsibility to God falsely believe if they just deny that God exists then He can't blame them for their part of the events that happened that day on a hill in Jerusalem. If God doesn't exist, then certainly (they think) Jesus was just a man. No God, No Son. We know better. *Denial* is a punishable sin and will not be forgiven if not rectified through salvation before a person dies.

To satisfy the mind, when a person commits a transgression, they may make a last-ditch effort to satisfy their need for forgiveness by doing some good deeds for the offended. That does not make everything well'. It is the right thing to do of course, but all transgression against another person original from sin against God. In other words, when we sin against any other person, that sin is disgraceful to God and against God. Being forgiven by another person is not the same as being forgiven by God. To be forgiven by someone who has been hurt makes one feel better, temporarily, but no sacrifice other than Jesus will wash a sin away. We have nothing of worth to sacrifice God knew we all would sin, and a sinner can't forgive sin, especially not his own. The price must be paid. There was no other way than for the sacrifice to be Holy and there is only One Holy enough to offer the sacrifice. Has Jesus been your accepted sacrifice?

Jesus is the Lover of your Soul, who is He to you?

RAP = Read And Pray

Journal your chosen Scriptures below.
List book, chapter and verses:

_____
_____
_____
_____
_____
_____
_____
_____
_____
_____
_____

Write out your prayer for these Scriptures below:

_____
_____
_____
_____
_____
_____
_____
_____
_____
_____
_____
_____
_____

(Bonus points = 500 page)

RAP = Read And Pray

Doodle Page

Finish the Drawing below.
Then at the bottom of this page write out your personal testimony about

Who Jesus is to you?

___

___

Jesus is my:

___
___
___
___
___
___
___

(Bonus points = 500 page)

86

RAP = Read And Pray

First Steps After Salvation

There are certain things to do as soon as possible after a person is saved that will enhance spiritual growth and is very pleasing in the sight of God.

#1. Be baptized.
#2. Join and attend a Bible Believing local Church for discipline and fellowship.
#3. Remember Jesus' sacrifice by partaking of the Lord's Supper.

While being baptized is not a commandment to satisfy salvation' possession; it is, however, very important to the new Christian's growth in faith. Baptism before salvation is like a farmer putting the cart before the horse because the cart cannot pull itself. Having the cart is nice but it cannot move without some other power to move it. And joining a church without having experienced salvation may put a name on a membership roll – just not the right one in heaven Many people join churches for a variety of reasons. That could be just because others in their circle join. Other reasons are that church membership may seem to be a prestigious, credibility entry on a resume', or part of a group of people with benefits of some sort. In such cases, the ink never dries. Baptism, church membership and partaking of the Lord's supper are reserved for soul-saved born-again believers in the power of Jesus' death, burial, and resurrection. Partaking of The Lord's Supper without believing in the Lordship of Jesus Christ is a dangerous act. It has no significant meaning to the unsaved and is mockery to the Trinity. Many play-church in these ways without being a part of The Church.

Judas became a part of the fellowship of disciples walking with Jesus, but Judas' heart was not right with God. Of course, Jesus knew this from the beginning, He was not shocked by Judas' betrayal. Since we do not have the benefit of insight like God does, it would be wrong to judge another's soul salvation. We should not ignore them or alienate those who seem to be imposters? We cannot take that logic if we go by Jesus' example. Of course, we know Judas was there to fulfill Scripture.

I live in the Bible-Belt of America and I've yet to see a perfect church and I know for sure when I join one that if it was perfect, it no longer is. Leave judgment to God and let Him guide you to a Church that preaches and teaches His Word under the anointment of a God-called preacher who obeys the Holy Spirit. That is as close to perfect as you are going to get. Join that church with the intent of using your God given talents and gifts to glorify God and advance His Kingdom. Then, all will be well with your soul. We have a purpose and commission from God on how to serve Him.

RAP = Read And Pray

> *Matthew 28:19-20*
> *"Go ye therefore, and teach all nations, baptizing them*
> *in the name of the Father, and of the Son, and of the Holy Ghost.*
> *Teaching them to observe all things whatsoever I have commanded*
> *you: and, lo, I am with you always,*
> *even unto the end of the world. Amen"*

The believer can grow in knowledge and understanding by spending time with God, listening to Him through His Word then communicating with Him in intimate prayer. This is the believer's part in the process of living holy in an unholy world. Having fellowship with other believer's means living on this earth just got a lot sweeter.

Baptism

Jesus was baptized by John and He came "*straightway out of the water*", then He saw "*the heavens opened, and the Spirit like a dove descended upon Him.*" Oh, - There's more. Right before His eyes something extraordinary happened: "*There came a voice from heaven saying, Thou art my beloved Son, in whom I am well pleased.*" (Mark 1:10-11). Wow! What a testimony of the importance of baptism!

Personally, I have been baptized three times. As a child I was baptized by my preacher/father because a friend told me if I loved Jesus then I had to be baptized to prove it. I was baptized the second time by my pastor/husband after being saved when I was twenty-seven years old. I was baptized for the third time in the Jordan River in Israel; - just because I could. The one that really matter was; the second.

Water alone does not save. The blood of Jesus Christ brings salvation, not water. Following the scripture and being baptized is important in spiritual growth as a public proclamation that the person is not ashamed to be counted as a born-again believer. It is also important to spiritual growth because Jesus did it and it pleased God.

Church Membership

Jesus liked reading the scriptures at church. But all the attendees did not like him. Furthermore, He knew some hearts were not right with God. He went anyway. At age 12 He loved being in the Temple so much that He stayed behind when his family

RAP = Read And Pray

left to go home. *"And it came to pass, that after three days they found him in the temple, sitting in the midst of the doctors, both hearing them, and asking them questions. And all that heard him were astonished at His understanding and answers."* Luke 2:46-47

Why did He stay behind in the temple?
"How is it that ye sought me? Wist ye not that I must be about my Father's business?" Luke 2:49

He was about His Father's business. Jesus went to church not to see or be seen but because He was about His Father's business.

Jesus did it and it pleased God.

The Lord's Supper

Jesus initiated the Lord's Supper, because He is the LORD. *Luke 22:19-20 "And he took bread, and gave thanks, and brake it, and gave unto them, saying, This is my body that is given for you: this do in remembrance of me. v. 20 Likewise also the cup after supper, saying, This cup is the new testament in my blood, that is shed for you."*

In this subtle way He was telling the disciples what was about to happen. His body would be broken like the bread and His blood would come pouring out like a drink. Participating in the Lord's Supper is a joyful privilege found in a somber moment of remembering what Jesus did on the Cross of Calvary. Only those who have been washed in His blood are worthy to take this sacrament. Jesus initiated it as a way for us to remember His sacrifice and with the purpose of unity among brothers and sisters in Christ.

Jesus did it and it pleased God.

The New Testament of that Jesus spoke was being recorded verbatim by those who were inspired by God to write such under the direction of the Holy Spirit. The people had a need to know the when, why, and how's of the final sacrifice and they needed fellowship that would require lots of discipline. Following these ordinances will be a great blessing to your spiritual walk with God. The Ten Commandments are still God's Word as is the entire Bible. The 31,102 verses are true. Set your goal to

RAP = Read And Pray

Read and Pray every verse. If you do not have a Church Family, use this time to reflect on and take this opportunity to set it as a priority for the near future.

"Let us hold fast the profession of our faith without wavering;
(for He is faithful that promised;)
and let us consider one another to provoke
unto love and to good works:
not forsaking the assembling of ourselves together,
as the manner of some is; but exhorting one another:
and so much the more, as ye see the day approaching."
Hebrews 10:23-25

Have you been baptized? _____Yes _____No
If yes, describe how this made you feel: If no, why not?

Have you joined a Bible Believing/Bible Teaching Church? _____Yes _____No
If yes, list some benefits you enjoy as a member. If no, why not?

Do you participate in the ordinance of the Lord's Supper? _____Yes _____No
If yes, what does this ordinance mean to you? If not, why not?

Comment below why each of these things are important to spiritual growth:

(Bonus points = 500 page)

RAP = Read And Pray

On the following two pages list some of the things you have learned from Chapter 3:

RAP = Read And Pray

Chapter 4
Prayer

RAP = Read And Pray

What does it mean to Pray?

Read John 14-17

Prayer is without doubt the greatest honor a Christian will ever have while on earth. Just to think we can commune directly with the God of all creation is mind-blowing. Yet, this great honor is often misunderstood and unused. While praying silently is one thing and can bless the heart; praying as a warrior in armor before a living God is yet a totally different experience. Thinking is not the same as praying. When a person "thinks" they are actually trying to reason *with oneself* but when a person prays (audibly or silently) the focus should always be on the One to whom they are speaking.

Prayer according to an ordinary dictionary can mean anything from 'meditation' to 'chant'. It is also used by some to mean "a solemn request for help or expression of thanks addressed to God *or an object of worship.*" People can go all their adult lives requesting prayer from others without knowing how to pray for themselves. If others are "praying" then that indicates there may be some sort of action toward hope. Hope is the one thing that gives all peoples in all places a sense of relief. Where hope is there is also a flicker of light in the darkest of souls. Hope is hearing the birds sing pre-dawn - even before the light of day. The singing birds must feel the release of darkness even while in the dark. Let me emphasis that *prayer to God is not a mindless chant nor is it effective/satisfying/comforting when done toward another person or any object.* When a person asks for prayer, they want you to petition on their behalf and talk to *The One* who can actually satisfy all needs.

Furthermore, people are carnal beings and all things are objects that were created outside themselves or their own power. Bodies and objects wear out and are consumable commodities that will be distorted by time and will not be ever-present. Objects are stationary and not moveable under their own power and can disappear, be used up or destroyed. Therefore anything other than God Almighty that is *worshipped or prayed* to is an imposter and not worthy of worshipful praise. No object or being, is always presence or all-knowing nor is any object or person all powerful. On the contrary, only God Almighty, is worthy of praise and worship in prayer. Peace with God is only accessible through Jesus Christ, His Son.

Learning to pray is as easy as carrying on a conversation with a dear friend. When I answer my phone I expect the person calling to identify themselves immediately. Likewise, when I make a call, the first thing I want to do is simply identify myself to the person who answers the phone. I want them to know who they are talking to. Jesus liked that procedure also because in instructing the disciples to pray the first thing He told them was to pray:

RAP = Read And Pray

"Our Father who art in heaven".

To begin a prayer in this manner says two things:

1. The words *Our Father* tells God that I am one of His children.
2. This statement also identifies God as my Father who resides in heaven and by acknowledging God as *Father* immediately indicates that there is a real and personal relationship with Him.

This simply acknowledgment often changes what I say next because I want to let God know that not only is He my Father, but He is also the creator of all things and nothing is impossible with God. Recognizing this makes me think more carefully what I might say in my petition of prayer. This is not to be considered as timidly praying, but rather boldly confident in His ability to grant above and beyond our wildest dreams of good things He wants to shower on His children. Things such as indescribable joy and heart calming peace. Those two things alone could throw me into a time of hallelujah praise, just knowing of His extreme agape, unconditional love for me, His child.

Prayer is not words spoken to the air; prayer has a target and the goal is to pray directly into the divine will of God, that is the best place to live and work. Let me say again, living and working in God's divine will is the best place to be because it is there that we find the best of everything life has to offer. We can settle for God's permissive will but that is not His design for a successful meaningful life while on earth. Doing things my way falls short of the bullseye, even though I will hit the target. We should study the difference in God's permissive will up against the light of His divine will.

Fellowshipping with God goes further. Fellowshipping with God breaks bearers. True, He readily recognizes the relationship when we call on his name in prayer; but how much do we linger in fellowship with Him by listening as He speaks. God hears and answers those with whom He has a personal, intimate, relationship and fellowship with and His answers always come from the heart of a true loving Father.

How can a person pray to God when they are alienated from Him? When they have not as yet, acknowledged Him to be all-knowing, ever-present, and all powerful, then why bother? The greatest blessing for an unbeliever is to have a Christian friend who is interceding for him or her.

A woman whose husband was unfaithful and causing her much torment was still walking in unsettled waters after the divorce. She was trying to get pass the pain he had caused but

RAP = Read And Pray

he was still unrepentant. She told me that during her prayer time she had started asking God to "bless her husband".

I asked her why she would do that? She could only answer that she didn't want anything bad to happen to him. God has never wanted evil to be blessed. In her case praying blessings on a sinful, unrepentant person is praying amiss. God does not want to bless the sinner in his sin. God wants to save the sinner into righteousness. That is the blessing all unsaved people need and is what we should pray for.

"Blessed are ye, when men shall revile you, and persecute you, and shall say all manner of evil against you falsely, for my sake. Rejoice, and be exceeding glad: for great is your reward in heaven: for so persecuted they the prophets that were before you." Matthew 5:11-12

As a Christian there is a responsibility to always uphold the truth, even in times of persecution. We have a responsibility to stand tall, amidst sinful arrows meant to destroy us because we are the salt of the earth and a light in a dark world where bad is called good; and good is called bad. The world needs to see the difference in us so we need to walk fearless and courageous in this world because the battle is already won. Trust God to handle every situation that satan meant as a way to dishonor God. Satan's attacks have one purpose and that is to hinder God's work because He knows He cannot stop it and the easiest way for him to do that is to silence God's children by backing them into a corner. *Nobody, not even satan, has power to put God's children in a corner!*

What are some benefits of prayer?

*Prayer is a difference maker.
*Prayer is a solace.
*Prayer is a relief giver.
*Prayer is fellowship.
*Prayer is a burden lifter.
*Prayer is hope.
*Prayer is a life-line.
*Prayer is victory.

If you need a difference, if you need a solace, if you need relief, if you need fellowship, if you need a burden lifter, if you need hope, if you need a life-line to victory and if you are a Christian; you have access to all these things. God takes the initiative in instigating His will. It is up to the individual to pray, listen and obey and to know how to respond to God's invitation for involvement in His plan. He is already at work, and we should join Him in what

He is doing rather than beg and plead with Him to bless what we are doing. Being in God's will is not waiting, worrying and wondering what His will is but rather it is about living in His will daily, by being in fellowship with Him constantly in order to know how and when to join Him in what He is already doing. This way, we don't have to pray for Him to come over here where we are to straighten out the mistakes we might make by taking matters into our own hands.

It is much better to live in God's divine will than to just pop in occasionally. In such a case, He must align our will to match His. This process can be somewhat painful, but necessary.

Prayer Umbrellas

When The Holy Spirit is interceding for me, I am under the security of a *prayer umbrella* that has me covered. Visualize it. Storms are raging, lightening is flashing, and torrential rain is falling. Despite being in the midst of your storm , there you are dancing joyfully under the umbrella you do not hold. In addition to the Holy Spirit's intercession, other Christians have you covered when you cannot voice the words yourself. There is great comfort in intercessory prayer because there are times when you hold the umbrella for others and times when other have you covered under their prayer umbrella.

Some of the most difficult storms of life come with the death of loved ones. I have been called to say an earthly good-by to my mother, father, husband, granddaughter, two sisters, four brothers, nephews, a still-born niece and in-laws whom I loved dearly. Not to mentions friends as close as my own brothers and sisters. Some days my sadness and grief was so great I could not pray. It was my turn to sit in the grief seat. When my parents were gone I wondered who would then intercede for me daily? Who was praying for me when I stood beside the bedside of my son who was on life-support not knowing if he would have another tomorrow? I needed someone to hold a prayer umbrella over me so I had to trust God to instruct the Holy Spirit to whispered my name into a prayer warrior's heart. And He did.

After my husband died, I didn't ask God for a second husband who would love me unconditionally; yet He gave me one. Coming closer to the end of my life than I am to the beginning I've seen God's faithfulness *all my life*. He has winked at me so often in ways only He knew of my heart's desire. Even when those desires were never voiced, He saw my heart and delivered.

God will confirm who He is in lots of ways but let me add – don't make Him prove it. He knows where you are headed and if it is in the wrong direction then He may allow some very tough days and miserable conditions (in love for your soul) to bring you back on the

RAP = Read And Pray

right track. That's what a loving Father does. God delights in doing for us what only God can do.

Describe a time when you have been under another person's *prayer umbrella*:

Praying without ceasing?

To pray without ceasing means our mind, heart, soul and actions stay on the truths of God's all knowing, all powerful and ever presence in us and around us as we fellowship with Him daily. (Read 1 Thessalonians 5:16-28)

Write out below your own definition of what it means to *pray without ceasing*.

RAP = Read And Pray

The Beauty of The Lord's Prayer

Petition	God's Purpose/Instruction	Meaning
"Father in Heaven Hallowed be Thy Name"	He is Holy, He is our creator, He has all authority, and He is our loving Father.	The 1st three points directly concern God and His person of being the one true God of all time. We must realize who we are talking to.
"Thy will be done on earth as it is in heaven"	We must realize God has all authority and must surrender to His will. Then be willing to accept His divine will.	Don't pray (backwards) *for your will to be done on earth and for God's will to be done only in Heaven.*
"Give us our daily bread"	God is good and the giver of all that is good. He knows what we need and gives abundantly so we may have *to give*, not keep.	"Bread" as used here comes from the Greek word that represents not just food, but every physical thing we need.
"Receive forgiveness to grant forgiveness."	Share mercy. God is the God of forgiveness and grace. Through His love, we can love and have power to forgive.	God is merciful and He demands us to be merciful also. He expects us to share what we have received. The power to fully forgive comes only from God.
"Lead us not into temptation."	God's purpose is for our protection. His instruction is to realize temptations of disobedience does not come from Him. He is Holy.	We pray for protection and power to be overcomers while living in a sinful world. This power comes from Christ Jesus.
"Deliver us from the evil one."	God shields us from being consumed by evil influence. He desires for us to be in fellowship with Him and other believers through worship and praise.	God's own Son was tempted; therefore He understands we need His constant help. We can be confident conquerors through Jesus Christ.

For Thine is the Kingdom, the power and the glory forever, Amen.

RAP = Read And Pray

On this page, in your own words describe the beauty of the Lord's Prayer and what it means to you personally:

RAP = Read And Pray

Praying the Lord's Prayer

Matthew 6:9-13 and Luke 11:2-4

Jesus's disciples saw Him pray many times. They surely noticed that there was a strong connection between Jesus' prayers and the power He showed in every aspect of His life. By watching Him pray, they learned a lot about what happens when a person prays in faith to the Heavenly Father. Not once did Jesus instruct them to pray to Him. He always pointed them to His Father in heaven. Since Jesus had a need to pray then how much more needful is it for a Christian to humbly seek God in prayer? Jesus realized this need so not only did He pray for His disciples and the world; but He also prayed for us alive today and the world in that we live.

> *"Neither pray I for these alone, but for them also that shall believe on me through their word." John 17:20*

It is of extreme important that a Christian read and re-read the <u>14-15-16 and 17th chapters of John</u> for clarity concerning the Trinity and Prayer. These chapter were written by John when he walked with our Lord. He was able to quote verbatim Jesus' comments, teachings and instructions in a timeless manner that applies (especially applies) to our world in 2024 and beyond as long as the earth stands as is. I would encourage everyone to read these four chapter on a regular basis because it is the solution to alleviate depression and anxiety. Once a person truly understands God's intent and Jesus' obedience to God's divine will, then understanding our need for the indwelling Holy Spirit comes into clear view. Jesus did not leave us helpless or hopeless with His ascension.

Anytime, and I repeat – "anytime" I find myself anxious or distressed, it is because I forget who I am in light of Who Jesus is and I've let down my guard by neglecting daily personal Bible study and prayer.

Jesus exhibited the how, when and where concerning praying as His disciples watched and learned. They did not know that they would be granted similar powers concerning healing and miracles. The day would too soon come that they would not see Jesus's face nor hear His word and that was ok because Jesus did not intend to leave them hopeless or fearfully abandoned.

> John 14:18: *"I will not leave you comfortless: I will come to you."*
> 1 Samuel 12:22 says, *"For the LORD will not forsake His people for His great name's sake: because it hath pleased the LORD to make you His people."*

RAP = Read And Pray

There are many Scriptures in the Bible which should comfort us as we know that He knows all about us and that should not be a fearful thought. God loves us not because of who we are, but rather in spite of who we are, for we are just sinners who have been saved by grace.

Psalms 139: 1-4 "O LORD, thou hast searched me and known me. Thou knowest my downsitting and mine uprising, thou understandest my thought afar off. Thou compassest my path and my lying down, And art acquainted with all my ways. For there is not a word in my tongue, But, lo, O LORD, thou knowest it altogether."

Consider this: If God already knows everything about us then why is it so hard to confess our sins? The fact is we don't want to confess our sins because that means we own up to it and thereby we must face the consequences. Let's keep in mind that we don't *become* guilty when we confess, we confess because we are already guilty.

The Lord's Prayer is a beautiful outline of how to pray. God likes for us to be specific in prayer even though He is a very good interpreter and knows exactly what the heart is trying to say when we have difficulty finding the right words. His outline found in Matthew 6 and Luke 11 covers all things such as God's holiness and sovereignty, as well as His authority. It also give space for us to pray for mercy, protection and deliverance.

Jesus's teaching in light the Lord's prayer is for the Christian to create intimacy and fellowship with His Father, and to do this first; then to pray for oneself. After intimacy and fellowship with our creator is established, freedom comes to pray for others in effective intercession. Starting prayer time by simply praising God for who He is will result in changes of prayer petitions. It is possible to be more concerned about God's will than any suggestions we might offer Him in how to handle our requests.

Another point that needs to be made before we study an outline for prayer in light of the example of the Lord's Prayer, is to remember God is not shocked or surprised by anything said to Him. He knows you even better than you know yourselves and desires for you to pray as the unique individual He created. Come into His presence confident that He already understands your situation and He has a divine plan for your future. You see, nothing has ever 'just occurred' to Him and He has never been shocked or afraid. He is all knowing, all powerful and ever-present. God is "Omniscient" (All Knowing) "Omnipotent" (All Powerful) and "Omnipresent" (Ever Present).

Praying without ceasing becomes a way of life. Praying under the leadership of the Holy Spirit turns problems into triumphs and happens when trusting in the Almighty to do what only the Almighty can do. Overcomers thank God for both good times and bad.

RAP = Read And Pray

2 Corinthians 12:9-10: "And He said unto me, My grace is sufficient for thee: for my strength is made perfect in weakness. Most gladly therefore will I rather glory in my infirmities, that the power of Christ may rest upon me. Therefore I take pleasure in infirmities, in reproaches, in necessities, in persecutions, in distresses for Christ's sake: for when I am weak, then am I strong."

Desire to deepen your prayer time with fellowship with God. The results will be a closer walk with Him.

"Just A Closer Walk With Thee"
I am weak but Thou art strong
Jesus Keep me from all wrong
I'll be satisfied as long
As I walk, let me walk close to Thee

Just a closer walk with Thee
Grant it, Jesus, is my plea
Daily walking close to Thee
Let it be, dear Lord, let it be.

(Songs with similar chorus lyrics were published in the 1800s, including lyrics by Martha J. Lankton (a pseudonym for Fanny Crosby) and music by William Kirkpatrick, that was published in 1885. Some references in Kansas credit an African-American foundry worker.)

RAP = Read And Pray

Effective prayer

The effectual fervent prayer of a righteous man availeith much. James 5:16

Prayer, being the highly intimate and extremely personal thing that it is; shows it effects on a person's soul as well as universally and all the way to heaven's gates while connect soul to soul and at the same time massaging the very heart of God. Furthermore, prayer is capable of bringing down false authority that throw lies to the wind hoping these lies fall, as if from heaven, into the homes and hearts of the deceivable who wait for something or someone to falsely justify their self-righteousness. Prayers of the righteous intercept these missiles of deceitful, exhausting the efforts of undermining God's standards of holiness by exposing lies which turn them to rubble because truth exalts the true sovereign living God. The effectual fervent prayer of the righteous yields results. In plain words, it is prayer and communion with God, the creator of all things, that changes things from impossible to *'done'*. The enemy uses every pick and shovel available to dig potholes of falsehood, but God can use only His Word to part seas.

So then, 1) What has happened to churches across our nation who are crumbling inside their own clay walls? 2) Where are the courageous leaders of authority and the strong family units or do they even still exist? 3) Is there such a thing as transparency that can see through and maneuver over hurdles of lies in order to see truth?

The answers to these question may appear discouraging but there are still courageous people who embrace honesty and wear the whole armor of God and there are still Churches (congregations of the saved by grace) who know the power of prayer as God ordained it to be. On the flipside satan has found fertile faulty thinking minds full of untruths to cultivate his purposes both inside and outside the church realm. If God's people who are saved slide into heaven by the seat of their pants, then where do the sinners and unforgiven stand?
Be no deceived; God is not mocked: for whatsoever a man soweth, that shall he also reap. Galatians 6:7

All sin shall be exposed and the blanket lifted which has been put over sin and unholiness. No covering hides anything from God for its invisible anyway, to God. Totally useless. Pretensive and ineffective. Wasted time. God knows if the one praying is a child of His or not. If so, then He is ready to have the person praying crawl up into His lap for some me-and-you time. If the person praying is not one of His, then He is still waiting to hear the sinner's prayer of repentance.

RAP = Read And Pray

Personally, I have no doubt that God blessed me before I became a Christian and I saw Him working in and around me for His purpose. However, I take no credit for those blessings received as anything to do with my part in the equation. I am confident that my godly mother

and other Christians who were praying for me and on my behalf with the main goal being bringing me to the saving grace of Jesus Christ. As a matter of fact, after my mother passed away when I was twenty years old I wondered, "who can I depend on to pray for me now?" Seven years later I was saved. When my daddy died in 1994 I wondered the same thing but this time, I knew it was my responsibility to pray for myself.

It is a very good thing when other Christians pray for us; but that does not compare in any way to the thrill of being able to come into God's presence oneself as a sinner saved by grace who God welcomes into His presence as His child. Once a person has their sins forgiven by the sacrifice of Jesus Christ who was under the obedience of God the Father for the remission of sin, then life begins. The life of a new-birth. All things are new and the old considered way of life becomes only a memory as the new way of life shows itself to be full of truth, mercy and grace which results in wanting to spend time with God the Father, because the Son, Jesus Christ, has covered sin with no evident of it ever existing. This experience is joy unspeakable and full of glory and the very reason we are born in the first place.

You see, God wants every soul to fellowship with Him because there is one thing that God needs and desires that He can get from no place other than from you and nobody else can do it for you. That is: Your worship and praise. Yes, you were created to love your Creator. He needs, desires and wants to have an intimate fellowship with you. That's called prayer while here on this earth and is called peace forevermore when in heaven.

God is all knowing, all powerful and ever present; but, He has placed one restriction upon Himself that He will not and cannot do. He did this when He gave us free-will to choose. While He loves each of us unconditionally with agape love; He will not make us love Him back. He gave up this right by not creating us as puppets on a string to obey His ever desire. He wants us to willingly love Him back with a new heart of love.

If prayer is lacking or unimportant or unanswered for you, then please ponder these things and find out why. It is so vital for us, as Christians, to have an understanding of the Trinity and God's design for happiness on earth and joy in heaven. Having peace with God is the purpose of the journey. When we come to the age of accountability we stand in the blood of Jesus Christ with a need to pray. We have a choice to either stomp in this sacrifice or to walk through it to victory and salvation.

RAP = Read And Pray

Something is wrong in my prayer life and worship of God if it has to be jumpstarted by someone else's praise. And something is wrong with my faith if it can be silenced by someone's else opposition. Being sanctified after salvation does not mean going through life alone and hoping for the best. On the contrary, It means the Holy Spirit is always on hand and that God is working on us to teach us how to pray, worship and fellowship with Him while we are on earth. It's a prelude to full time worship in heaven.

There was a time I stood on the wrong side of the fence and other times I tried to straddle it but I cannot blame that on anyone but myself. I had to finally realize there is no fence. A person is never nearly saved or nearly lost; it's a definite, one or the other.

Go ahead and say what is on your heart to God. You will not shock Him. And it will not change His love for you. He doesn't love you because you might be good as gold; on the contrary, He loves you even when actions mocked Him. He is a lot more patient with us than we are with others. He just keeps loving and waiting because He knows what we need is the Lord. God the Father, Jesus the Son, and the ever-present Holy Spirit. But keep this one thing in mind, the day will come when you will take a knee in His presence.

Let's determine to take time to exercise our prayer life which will make us strong and able to stand even when we are weak.

Confess your faults one to another and pray one for another that ye may be healed. The effectual fervent prayer of a righteous man availeith much. James 5:16

And if the righteous scarcely be saved, where shall the ungodly appear? 1 Peter 4:18

But we are all as an unclean thing, and all our righteousness are as filthy rages; and we all do fade as a leaf; and our iniquities, like the wind, have taken us away. Isaiah 64:6

RAP = Read And Pray

The Holy Spirit's part in prayer:

Likewise the Spirit also helpeth our infirmities:
for we know not what we should pray for as we ought:
but the Spirit itself maketh intercession for us
with groanings which cannot be uttered. Romans 8:26

Honestly, without the Holy Spirit's guidance I would be as lost as a ball in high weeds in even starting a prayer to God. I need the third person of the Trinity. He reads me. Then He interrupts what He discovers, translating it on my behalf in terms I don't know how to say. (Just another bonus of being a Christian.) Do I have to understand all there is to know about the Holy Spirit before He works in my life. Absolutely not. It's ever-learning.

My friend, Robin, shared how she taught her children about the Holy Spirit by using the example of water. Water can appear by taking on three forms. 1) Liquid, 2) vapor/steam, 3) frozen as a solid object. All three consist of one thing – water. Another example is that of wind. Wind is an invisible force and a thing that leaves its mark wherever it goes.

The Holy Spirit has a major part in prayer because guidance of the Holy Spirit is where the person praying gets counsel and leadership in knowing when, how, where and what to pray. It takes a little practice to become aware of the ever-dwelling Holy Spirit inside our souls. It's difficult to explain but easy to recognize. Rev. George Donald Graham explained this very well in a sermon he preached at Eastside Baptist Church on October 20, 2024. The following is a synopsis of that sermon as told by this author and witnessed by our congregation. This edited version is used by permission.

RAP = Read And Pray

The Wind of the Holy Spirit
By Bro. George Donald Graham

The Text
The wind bloweth where it listeth, and thou hearest the sound thereof, but canst not tell when it comes, and whither it goeth: so is everyone that is born of the Spirit. (John 3:8)

We cannot see this wind as it moves and it cannot be explained other than by the revelation of the Holy Spirit as God directs Wind can come as a gentle breeze of refreshment or in a mighty storm such as drives a tornado or hurricane.

There are certain facts about this wind generated by the Spirit of God.

1. It is not good when no wind is blowing.
2. Wind has a will of its own.
3. Wind needs no permission where it goes.
4. People know where it is because of its effects.
5. There has never been a time when the Spirit was not working.
6. This wind blows in different ways.
7. Wind can be refreshing or devastating.

The wind of the Holy Spirit is the key to all we do in service to God because it is His leadership that directs us. This wind cannot be tamed or cornered and cannot be predicted. It blew at just the right time for Jesus to use it as an example of the Holy Spirit when He was talking to a man named Nicodemus. In the third chapter of John in the New Testament Jesus explained what it means to be born again to Nicodemus who could not understand how a person could enter into their mother's womb again. His understanding was totally carnal. Jesus used the example of literal wind, which we all have experienced throughout our lifetimes as its moves in different ways upon earth, to help Nicodemus see that people who have never been born-again cannot feel the Holy Spirit's leadership.

There are many Scriptures in the Bible that refer to the Holy Spirit's movement. Too many to mention them all. One of them directly concerned the new Church age in which we live.

In the second chapter of Acts in the Bible, the wind of the Spirit began to move in a new way on the day of Pentecost.

And when the day of Pentecost was fully come, they were all with one accord in one place. And suddenly there came a sound from heaven as of a rushing mighty wind, and it filled all the house where they were sitting. (Acts 2:1-2)

RAP = Read And Pray

Prayer is basic to a new birth. To know God you must have movement of the Holy Spirit. As the wind blows so does the Spirit of God. Meteorologist exhaust many efforts in understanding the cause and effect of wind's movement and although they can come pretty close in prediction of earthly wind, the wind of the Holy Spirit is far beyond mankind's efforts to explain because God is in total control of both. For the wind of the Holy Spirit to work in a person's life, they must raise the sail.

Just to show how the wind of the spirit of God has always been, we will look at the beginning of the Bible in Genesis, to the back of the Bible in Revelation and then to the middle of the Bible in the book of Psalms for evidence of the Holy Spirit's presence.

In the beginning God created the heaven and the earth.
And the earth was without form, and void; and darkness was upon the face of the deep.
And the Spirit of God moved upon the face of the waters. (Genesis 1:1-2)

And the Spirit and the bride say, Come. And let him that heareth say, Come.
And let him that is athirst come. And whosoever will,
let him take the water of life freely. (Revelation 22:17)

Whither shall I flee from thy presence? If I ascend up into heaven, thou art there:
If I make my bed in hell, behold, thou art there. If I take the wings of the morning,
and dwell in the uttermost parts of the sea; Even there shall thy hand lead me,
and thy right hand shall hold me. (Psalms 139:7-10)

Think on these things during your quiet time and ponder on the truth of God's word. Sure God was present at the creation but so was Jesus and the Holy Spirit. The Bible clearly states that *the Spirit* of God moved upon the face of the waters. And God said, Let *us* make man in our image. (Genesis 1:26)

How did it all start?

Perhaps God looked at Jesus and said:

"Jesus, here is the deal. You will need to go to earth at some time. I know the people given a choice will choose the wrong way and be sinful. Sin must be punished. The only way for Us to restore them is through a spotless blood sacrifice. You will be a man, just as you are also My Son. It will be necessary for you to live with them and teach them but your carnal body will have to die. When it does, I will have to turn my back on you. You will be their sacrifice for their sins. Are you willing to do that?"

Jesus's focus has always been to do the Father's will. God was straight up with Him and Jesus was fully aware He would be called to die a humanly horrible death in order to satisfy the Father's plan. Jesus understood the plan for salvation and that He would be their free sacrifice for sin. He was willing yet when the time came for his bodily sacrificial offering, He prayed to God for another way if it was possible.

> *Father, if thou be willing, remove this cup from me: nevertheless not my will, but thine, be done. (Luke 22:42)*

Perhaps then God turned to the Holy Spirit which was moving upon the face of the waters and said:

"Holy Spirit, this involves You also. I am going to birth a church of people who will willingly return love to me as I have loved them first. They will be carnal but saved by grace and mercy. There will be no way they can stand alone and you will need to blow refreshing wind upon them for guidance and direction. After Jesus' resurrection, you will need to appear so they will know they are not alone. Are you willing to do that?"

The Holy Spirit had no problem with that because His existence was always to magnify the Father and the Son – not himself. The wind loves to hear instruction from God and quickly obeys, no questions asked. You see, God did not need us, He wanted us. That is why He sent the Holy Spirit to work with us and direct us.

Church are you blowing?
Is there movement in you?

Years ago I pastored a church of forty-two members and when I arrived the first thing I noticed was there was no wind blowing. God first dealt with problems that prevented the wind of the Holy Spirit from blowing. I don't like being in a place where the wind of the spirit is not moving, do you? People must allow the Holy Spirit to work and when this started happened people started obeying and being saved. This church grew rapidly after that.

The wind of the Spirit knows without His presence in the church there is no freedom, no joy, no happiness. No one will be saved or lives be changed. In such a place there is all rules and no liberty. Without the movement of the Spirit theology can contain us and the wind will just blow right by and leave you. That is not God's idea for His Church.

Put your sails up into the wind and don't be bound by your own opinions and thinking. Instead of just thinking about God, start praying to Him. Invite the Trinity to be welcome in your life and home.

The apostle Paul was the greatest missionary ever on earth. He understood the working and power of the Holy Spirit. Paul preached and things started happening. Not because Paul was high and mighty, but because he was standing in the wind of the Holy Spirit. If you don't want to change, God won't make you. Paul embraced his encounter with Jesus

RAP = Read And Pray

and was never the same again. The thing that changed Paul in the midst of his persecuting the Christians, was also the same wind recorded in Ezekiel 37:1-14 in a valley full of dry bones. If you have felt all dried up, then the wind needs to refresh you.

Then said He unto me, Prophesy unto the wind, prophesy, son of man,, and say to the wind, Thus saith the Lord GOD; Come from the four winds, O breath, and breathe upon these slain, that they may live. So I prophesied as He commanded me, and the breath came into them, and they lived, and stood up upon their feet, an exceeding great army.
(Ezekiel 37:9-10)

In closing, think how God might move you from where you are to a better place spiritually. Jesus obeyed God's plan, the Holy Spirit obeyed God the Father, and God wants you to be waken to His movement around you and in you. Turn your face to the wind of the Spirit and let it move you by opening your life to the influence of God's will. He will then do things you will not believe.

You must know that the Holy Spirit comes from God and is God. God uses people to help move you closer to Him by surrendering to His will. In your darkest night if you will open the window of your heart and listen, you will hear the wind. The Holy Spirit is not sleeping. He is working out God's purpose and God has a purpose for you.

Rev. George Donald Graham
As told by Brenda Kendrick

RAP = Read And Pray

Prayer Outline

The outline on the following page can be beneficial for training in how to use Scriptures during prayer time which relate to particular needs. God loves to hear His words repeated back to Him in prayer. There are four main divisions in this outline. 1) Recognizing the Trinty. 2) Acknowledging self. 3) Petitions and intercessions. 4) Worship and Thanksgiving.

Recognizing the Trinty, stresses the important of starting prayer with the acknowledgment to whom you speak. God is recognized as the creator of all things with special attention to His character. Coming into his presence with reverence and humility can change the entire prayer focus. Concentration is on God and His ability, rather than on problems and disabilities.

Acknowledging oneself as a sinner saved by grace opens up a time of realizing who we are in light of who God is and allows time for any needed confession of sins. In other words, clearing the air, so that intimacy in prayer can turn into fellowship with God renewing dedication by surrendering to God's sovereignty.

Petition and intercession may have changed than first expected when prayer begins with a time of acknowledging God as all powerful, all knowing and ever present. Things that were a great concern are turned from a state of worrisome to a pinnacle of hope and joy knowing all things are possible with God. Take time during intercession to be specific in your requests.

Finishing prayer time with praise, worship and thanksgiving lifts burdens and gives a great comfort of peace knowing God is a faithful father and will hear every prayer of His children. His desire is to bless His children abundantly above all we could think or ask. The beauty of intimacy with God is that He responds to a one sentence prayer such as *Jesus help me* as well as He does when hearing and answering an hour of prayer.

RAP = Read And Pray

Prayer outline example with Scripture references

I. The Trinity. 2 Corinthians 13:14
   A. God as the Creator of all things. Matthew 6:9
      1. God is Alpha and Omega. Revelation 22:13
      2. God is the Creator of all things. Genesis 1:1
   B. Attributes of *God*, The Father. Psalms 46:10
      1. God is Omniscient (all knowing). Psalms 69:5
      2. God is Omnipotent (all powerful). Psalms 29:4, Jeremiah 32:27
      3. God is Omnipresent (ever present). Psalms 139:2
   C. Mission of *Jesus*, The Son. Mark 1:1
      1. Jesus is the Son of God. Acts 9:20
      2. Jesus is the perfect spotless & holy sacrifice for sin. Hebrews 9:14
      3. Jesus is the link (door) to the Father. John 10:7
      4. Jesus's (death) blood sacrifice covers the sin of the repenting sinner. Philippians 2:8, 1 Corinthians 2:2, Hebrews 12:2
      5. Salvation (regeneration) hinges on the resurrection of Jesus. John 11:25-26, 1 Peter 1:3-5
   D. Counsel of the *Holy Spirit*. John 14:26
      1. The Holy Spirit (3rd person in Trinity) enables Christian to live holy in an unholy world. John 14:16-17
      2. The Holy Spirit intercedes on behalf of the Christian. Romans 8:26-27
      3. The Holy Spirit as indwelling comforter/counselor. John 14:18

II. Acknowledge *Self*. (Who you are in light of who God is.) Ephesians 2:8
   A. You are the person of your soul. Genesis 2:7,
   B. The soul will live forever. Luke 23:43, John 3:15-17, Romans 6:22-23
   C. Confess sins. Dead to Self. Alive in Christ Jesus. Proverbs 28:13, 1 John 1:9, 1 John 2:12, Acts 3:19, 2 Chronicles 7:14, Romans 6:11, Galatians 2:19-21, Romans 6:1-23, 1 Corinthians 15:22, 1 Peter 3:18
   D. Choose to live in God's perfect will. Romans 12:2, 2 Corinthians 13:11
   E. What does God require? Micah 6:8
   F. Sanctification happens from point of salvation to point of death. Leviticus 20:7, Joshua 3:5, 1 Thessalonians 5:23, 1 Thessalonians 4:3, Romans 12:2, Romans 6:22
   G. Commit to fellowship with a local Bible believing Church. Hebrews 10:25
   H. Using God's gifts and talents. 1 Corinthians 12:4-11, 1 Peter 4:10, Luke 11:13, 1 Peter 1:4-8, 1 John 2:27-28,

RAP = Read And Pray

    III.   Petitions & Intercessions. Romans 8:26-27, Ephesians 6:18,
               A. Personal prayer lists: James 5:16, 1 Thessalonians 5:25, Luke 6:28
1. Pray for wisdom to know how to respond to and witness to the lost that they may be saved. Make a prayer list of names who have not experienced salvation. Acts 2:38, James 3:17
2. Pray for friends and family. Philippians 1:3-6
3. Pray for your enemies. Matthew 5:44-48
4. Model Jesus' prayer. John 17
5. Pray for and help the poor. Matthew 19:21, Matthew 25:35-40 2 Corinthians 9:6-8
6. Ask for healing. 103:1-4, Psalms 107:19:22, Romans 9:14-17, Isaiah 53:5, 1 Peter 2:20-24, 2 Corinthians 6:1-10, Matthew 11:1-6, Philippians 4:29, Matthew 19:26, Mark 9:23, Luke 18:27, Mark 14:36
7. List your own personal requests below and look up related Scriptures:

_____
_____
_____
_____
_____
_____

    IV.   Close Prayer with worship and thanksgiving. Philippians 6:5-8, Psalms 40:5, Psalms 37:4-5, Proverbs 3:5-6

        A. Thank God for Jesus and saving grace.
        B. Praise God for the privilege of prayer and for answered prayers.
        C. Thank Him for all things – big and small, bad and good.
        D. Thank Him for miracles past and miracles to come.
        E. Thank Him for the person of the Holy Spirit as your comforter.
        F. Praise Him for He is worthy of all praise.
        G. Give God credit for all good things.
        H. Close prayer in the name of Jesus Christ and for His sake.

There is one thing God cannot get from anywhere else than from you.
*That is **your** praise and worship.*

RAP = Read And Pray

Prayer Example

The following is a sample of praying using the preceding outline, in part, and was recorded while working on a manuscript in my home office. I was not hidden in my closet at the time nor was I sitting in church during a moment of silence. It was a moment I needed to share with God who is ever present, all knowing and all powerful. I have selected a portion of that prayer to use as an example of fellowship with God, and *only* as an example. In no way is it intended to use as an override of being led to pray your way-your style under the direction of the Holy Spirit as He guides.

1. Acknowledge The Trinity

Lord God, you are alpha and omega – the beginning and end of all things. You always have been and always will be. You created the world, the worlds, the things seen and unseen. You can do anything, anytime, anywhere that you choose. You are all powerful. You are ever present. You are all knowing. You know me, you created me and placed me in my mother's womb. You are high above all known and unknown. God you are Holy. When I look up into the sky, I do not worship what I see; I worship what I know is beyond my sight. Right now I cannot see You as You are; but I can *know You* and I can feel You with just a glimpse.

Father, I did not see Jesus while He walked on this earth but many people alive in the day did. Some saw Him to be The Messiah and others did not know the truth and purpose of His presence: Because of their testimonies and your recorded Word I believe Jesus came to earth, as your Son, and He wanted us to know you in the same way He knew You, as a loving Father.

I confess Jesus to be my link to You. My salvation hinges on His resurrection. I come into your presence through prayer because I have been to the Cross of Calvary. Not to stand at the foot just to gaze upon it; but I have walked through His blood in a way to acknowledge my guilt. I admit God, I was there the day Your Son took that beating. Though not in the flesh, nevertheless I was there laying my stripe of sin upon His back. One of those blows of pain was for me. I was faced with the most important decision of my lifetime on April 21,1978. My soul search found me as one guilty of sin. Because of your forgiveness I have never felt more loved than I did on that day. I just basked in it, not understanding it all but thankful for it.

Jesus was willing to take punishment and pain He didn't deserve because that was your Plan for the perfect sacrifice for sin. Being human, as He was. I believe His mission on earth was simply to obey You and be the true example of obedience. Without Jesus' visit

RAP = Read And Pray

to the earth and His growing up experiencing all the emotions, circumstances, feelings, and tears – as a human – how could I know that You know how I feel? Oh, You know!

Jesus is the way to life eternal, without Him there is no remission for sin.

The day I accepted Jesus' sacrifice, I passed through to the other side receiving total security as a Child of the King. Your Child. I can now speak to you so humanly, without fear of your rejection because your Son's blood was not wasted. I gave You my messed-up life and all the guilt that was killing my soul; and You showered me with a wave of Agape love. The first gift you gave me was the gift of life as a living soul at my conception when you formed me in my mother's womb. The second gift was salvation, which I didn't deserve but you mercifully granted to me that secured my eternal home in heaven, but you were not done yet. The third gift was the indwelling of the Holy Spirit which enables me to live holy in an unholy world. All three of these gifts could come from nowhere except from you. Thank you!

2. Acknowledge self through confession and cleansing

Father, I have many things I need to talk to You about, but honestly, realizing I am now in your presence leaves me awe-struck and changes my prayer. I am in the most intimate place I have ever been. You know me. You know the inside and outside, the pretense and honesty. Help me to see me in the same light You see me. *Redeemed and a saved sinner*.

Please forgive me of all my sins. Help me to embrace that forgiveness and learn from my mistakes. I pray God that somewhere in my heart You find true worship. How can anyone describe the depth of peace that is freely given to the heart that holds nothing back from You? All I can say is "I surrender! You get all I got for as long as I got!" Right now, this very moment I'm Yours. You do with me as You will. Your presence is that powerful. I abandon myself. I am grateful for things You give me and that I see and witness, but it's not those things that I receive that are praiseworthy, *It is YOU.* You are God! You have revealed yourself to us through your Word and through your Son. For that, I am grateful. I praise You, my God! Thank you for your forgiving grace and mercy.

3. Petitions and Intercessions

I must come clean before You. It is so easy to self-justify my actions and reactions. I live here on a very sinful earth with temptations on every corner. But You know that already. Sometimes I wonder as The Spirit intercedes for me, if He reminds You what it is like living in a world surrounded by sinfulness. I am so foolish. You need no counsel.

I am reminded just now that you called me to be your Rep. I remember struggling in finding Your will in using any gift or talent you give, and You revealed to me to "just be My Rep."

RAP = Read And Pray

I don't put on a lapel button that says, "Jesus Representative", but I should always feel like one. I need help with that to be sure I don't miss any divine appointments.

Dear Father:
*_I plead_ for those who have hate in their hearts and who have never seen the truth of redemption. They are of all people most miserable. Open their eyes to the truth of Your love.

*_I pray_ for those who blame you for the bad things that happen to them. You should never be the One on trial. You are Good, _all the time_ You are Good.

*_I pray_ for you to be Glorified on earth as in Heaven.

*_I pray_ for my church family, that we all may be busy serving you in the way which would please you, using the talents and gifts You have shared with each one. May unity be present and evident in all decisions and brotherly love abundant.

*_I pray_ for my family and list them all by name and need…….
Most of all bless them with a knowledge of the simple truth of Your ever-present love and grant them each with abiding love one for another. Give them enough heart to care and resources enough to share. May each one treasure integrity and always be trust-worthy, courageous and honest.

*_I pray_ for freedom for our country and peace of Israel.

*_I pray_ for the sick – so many – and for widows and widowers. *I pray for the children who are without their parents and parents who are without their children.

*_I pray_ for leaders of our churches to be bold in the faith and strong in the spirit of truth.

*_I pray_ for those seeking You, may some Christian take the time to invest in them and share Your love in a way that their hearts will be open to the simple truth.

4. Worship and Thanksgiving.

I worship you now in heart and soul and with gratitude and thanksgiving. Teach me how to praise you in good times and bad times. Help me accept your answer to my prayers and that those answer will be in your time and in your way. I realize I will miss the best if I'm satisfied with your permissive will rather than your perfect divine will. I surrender my will to you to do as you please, for your glory and to advance your kingdom. Thank you for the _gift of peace_. I cannot live without it since I have experienced it. You will never take it from me; and satan cannot steal it away from me. Thank you for all Your blessings! In the name of Jesus Christ, and for His sake I pray. Amen

RAP = Read And Pray

*The wisdom that is from above is first pure,
then peaceable, gentle, and easy to be intreated,
full of mercy and good fruits,
without partiality and without hypocrisy.
James 3:17*

Now, ask for God's wisdom by inserting the above Scripture in your prayer and write out *your own prayer* below:

RAP = Read And Pray

Chapter 5
Sharing Jesus

Don't Miss the Mission

RAP = Read And Pray

Bread Baking and Sharing

"O taste and see that the LORD is good:
Blessed is the man that trusteth in Him."
Psalm 34:8

Salvation is more than a Recipe:

From my personal example, I was a church member since the age of eight and was teaching Sunday School as the pastor's wife for three years before I was saved by grace on April 21, 1978. I had head knowledge of Jesus but had never tasted the graciousness of God nor was I convinced that He truly loved me. Then one day He convinced my soul and pointed out that I was the one who didn't love Him. I wanted Him to accept me for who I was when in turn I had not been willing to accept Him for who He is. The thing about God's grace is He can always convict with His Word, even when the barrier of His Word is not one of His. There have been well known preachers who have been saved after they started preaching, some even preaching a long time.. Parishioners in the Churches who were saved from listening to these men were saved from listening to God's Word and obeying it; not from the power of the preacher who delivered the message.

It is estimated that only one-third of church members have been saved by grace before joining a Church. How sad is this? I was one of them up until that Friday on a spring day in 1978 when I went to my knees beside by bed and was regenerated.

After God gloriously saved my soul and I was born again, I wanted to share the love of God with others but really did not feel qualified. It had taken me a long time to follow the recipe or put the bread to the test by baking it in the oven and eating it. What good is a recipe if it has not been proven to be worth eating?

"And Jesus said unto them, I am the bread of life:
he that cometh to me shall never hunger;
and he that believeth on me shall never thirst." John 6:35:

Sharing Jesus takes courage and can be intimating until a person understands that the results is always up to God. Salvation happens when a person accepts Jesus as Savior. No one else is qualified to do this job. You, nor I, can save anyone' soul even if we were crucified in like manner as was Jesus. We would just be dead, and the world would still need a Savior. Likewise, the result from witnessing and sharing

Jesus in hopes that others will be saved is also in God's hands because He didn't call us to save anyone, He calls us to witness of the fact that He is the Bread of Life that satisfies. In soul winning the recipe is very simple. It is the application that we make hard. This entire book has one simple storyline; that is to be saved and know it. Then be obedient to God as He uses you in the way He sees fit to advance His Kingdom.

"For our rejoicing is this,
the testimony of our conscience, that in simplicity and
Godly sincerity, not with fleshly wisdom,
but by the grace of God,
we have had our conversation to you-ward."
2 Corinthians 1:12:

Salvation Plus Wisdom

Understanding of God's Word coupled with wisdom that comes from above is the greatest of all riches in this world.

"For the LORD giveth wisdom:
out of His mouth cometh knowledge and understanding."
"Happy is the man that findeth wisdom,
and the man that getteth understanding.
For the merchandise of it is better than the merchandise
of silver, and the gain thereof than fine gold."
Proverbs 3:13-14

Being a Christian means you have plenty of good and valuable things to share. If you have never shared Jesus with anyone just because you think you don't know how – then I beg you to reconsider. You are qualified to share Jesus because you know how you became a Christian. You know when and you know how you were saved so that fact alone qualifies you to share the Gospel with others, simply by verbalizing your own testimony. Just a few of the many excuses people shy away from sharing their personal salvation experience are; lack of bible study, failure to pray, faulty thinking, fear, not asking for Godly wisdom, and you name it. The one reason to share Jesus comes easily – it is a commandment.

RAP = Read And Pray

> *"Go ye therefore, and teach all nations,*
> *baptizing them in the name of the Father, and of the Son,*
> *and of the Holy Ghost:*
> *Teaching them to observe all things*
> *whatsoever I have commanded you: and, lo,*
> *I am with you always, even unto*
> *the end of the world. Amen."*
> Matthew 28:19-20

I enjoying telling my granddaughter on a bad hair day that she "can't mess up beautiful". And I've been known to tell my grandsons from time to time that they can't mess up "handsome" for to me that is who they are. To God, we are His children and when we try in obedience to do His will; He says – "you can't mess up when you obey."

Represent God

Sharing Jesus has nothing to do with me or you as far as the part of salvation, because we are only vessels God uses to do the work Himself. His toolbox has hammers, nails, flashlight, and cleaning rags. However, we look for the band aids to protect our own heart from guilt of making a mess of things. Jesus took the hammer and nails in order to shine The Light into the world and clean up the mess we created. He has no need for band-aids.

My missionary mother in Honduras knew how much I wanted to help talk someone to salvation. She helped me understand that salvation is not "talking someone through" to peace with God it's about representing God, then others can see Jesus in you. It's about letting the Holy Spirit have full reign of your dialogue. The many times I have shared Jesus since that day, I walk away not remembering what I said but I know how it happens when a person decides to trust in Jesus. It is because of their faith in God and certainly not because of me.

The next year on my mission trip to Honduras I sat at the 'prayer table' as person after person waited in line to find the simple message of the Gospel of Christ Jesus and be saved. I remember thinking after witnessing dozens of people being saved that: "this is what I was born for, no day will ever be better than this one." We all are born with such a purpose. Anything else is to settle for less instead of the best.

There is nothing more wonderful than helping someone understand the gospel and receive salvation by free acceptance. My prayer used to be that "I would *see* so and so be saved". It doesn't matter whether or not I actually see it. What matters

RAP = Read And Pray

is that it happens. While on the Billy Graham prayer team phone line sharing Jesus with someone sitting in their home thousands of miles away I could not see their faces at the moment. But there is just something about salvation that one can feel, even though salvation is not a feeling. It is the truth. The person whom He saves, He has power to keep. I've had more wonderful opportunities and experiences than one person should be entitled to, but none tops knowing God used me to point someone to Jesus.

That is what I hope for you as you study and be confident in God's Word and sure of your own salvation. Be ready to share Jesus.

Have you shared your testimony before? Why or why not?

Write some highlights about how God has worked in your life before:

How is God using you in current day to share Jesus with family, friends and or co-workers?

(Bonus points = 500 page)

RAP = Read And Pray

Servanthood

Entering servanthood begins the process of sanctification (which is covered in detail later in this study guide). There is one thing to take note of from the beginning, straight from salvations' gate/ The entire process of sanctification is all about servanthood. God did not save us so He could spend all His time correcting us from then on out. God saved us with the promise of His guidance all the way to heaven's pearly gates and that does not mean we can sit down and do nothing to advance His Kingdom from the point of salvation until the day we die. Let's not stress God with our complacency by having our focus centered on ourselves and our disabilities. God knows we are disabled in body and mind and that is why He embeds us with the Holy Spirit to pick up our slack. We give Him plenty of reason to shake his head and say, *when will they ever learn*?

If God wanted us to be perfect before He could use us then Jesus certainly would not have chosen the Disciples that He did. Think about it. Jesus chose selfish brothers who wanted to be the ones sitting closest to Him when they got to heaven (forget the others) and He chose a tax collecting cheater, a doubter and a thief. Stepping ahead to be named with these twelve disciples/apostles, Saul was chosen when he was on the way to arrest Christians for the purpose of prosecution. However, when Saul saw only the blinding light of holiness He became willing to leave his former life to make a complete turnabout. He learned how to serve because Jesus taught him how during his discipleship, first in isolation and then as a missionary spreading the gospel. Saul's name was changed to Paul and he was never that Saul again. Get this, after Paul was sent out to minister, only one of the disciple trusted him and that disciple-initiated acceptance by the others when he (Barnabus) stood up for Paul and his newfound identity: The rest is history. Today Paul is counted as The Apostle Paul, because he saw the risen Savior, Jesus.

Servanthood is the act of service freely given for the cause of Christ in obedience of and under the direction of the Holy Spirit. This is different from self-service because it usually will require sacrifice of some degree from the servant and sacrificial service is not convenient, costless or easy. However, it is the most rewarding and satisfying benefit involved in sanctifying the Christian because the results profit personal wellbeing, enhances enjoyment of life, creates happiness and emotional stability, as well as improves mental health. And servanthood grants, above all, spiritual strength and advances God's Kingdom. That is the gut of what being a Christian is all about.

Most Christians simply do not know where to begin their service for God. How can they, since there has not been any leadership from the Holy Spirit before being saved? This is where Church membership is so very important. Church is the place where service opportunities present themselves; if the church is following the leadership of the Holy Spirit. If a church has a mind of service then they will supply discipline and training, be mission minded, commit to community service, and offer regular opportunity inside the church family

RAP = Read And Pray

to support every area from infants in the cradle to homebound or those who are in elderly assistant living facilities.

Finally, servanthood is a commandment of the Lord to every born-again believer to *"Serve the Lord with gladness."* Psalms 100:2

Look up the following verses concerning servanthood and write them out on your note pages for reference: Psalms 2:11, Joshua 24:21, Colossians 3:24, Exodus 23:25, Romans 12:1-2, Romans 11:36, James 1:27, Joel 1:3, Proverbs 22:6, Luke 10:30-37.

Your Notes:

RAP = Read And Pray

Stages of Servanthood

What does it mean to be a Disciple?

The word disciple means to be a personal follower or student of a teacher, leader, or philosopher. When Jesus selected his twelve disciples they all became interns of the great physician and all but one would graduate with degrees and in three short years become capable of being ambassadors and representative of the Trinity consisting of, The Lord Jesus Christ, God His Father, and empowered by the Holy Spirit. Selected by and taught by Jesus during His ministry and being with Jesus on earth after His resurrection also qualified these men to be called Apostles. Paul would be added to this chosen group of Apostles and would call himself the least. (See 1 Corinthians 15:9)

Today Christians are being disciplined for service throughout life and there comes a time for us as well to step out of the boat and start serving God using the talents and gifts which He will provide. Just as Jesus first gave the disciples power, then commanded them to go-ye, He also instructed them where to go and what to do when they got there.

(Read Matthew 10)

Most of the disciples and especially the apostle Paul could have been called an Apostolic Ambassadors because they were missionaries or crusaders at heat.

What does it mean to be an Ambassador?

The moment we become Christians we are being disciplined and trained. While this discipleship ever continues there comes a turning point when we must start being the facilitator to train others. Noone is saved to 'keep the good stuff' but rather Christians are saved in order to share the good stuff. That being: the gospel of hope first, then materially as directed by the Holy Spirit. The word ambassador refers to a person who acts as a representative or promoter of a specified activity or an accredited diplomat sent by a country as its official voice. An ambassador for Christ is a Christian who represents Jesus and the Christian faith to the world. The term comes from 2 Corinthians 5:20. *"Now then we are ambassadors for Christ, as though God did beseech you by us: we pray you in Christ's stead, be ye reconciled to God*. This means that while He intercedes before the Father for us (Romans 8:34), we represent Him, bringing the kingdom of God to those around us who do not know Him yet. The disciples were given missions or particular jobs in order to branch out and get to work. Ambassadors use their strengths and God given talents and gifts in service to advance God's Kingdom. Those jobs may include preaching, local or foreign missions, teaching, visiting the sick, feeding the poor, etc. (See 1 Corinthians 7:20-24 and 1 Corinthians chapter 12)

RAP = Read And Pray

What does it mean to be a Representative?

Representatives

The difference in ambassadors and representatives is very simple. Representatives are on the job 24-7. That is twenty-four hours a day, seven days a week. None-stop. I was once very concerned about finding my talent and certainly didn't know where or how to be an ambassador until God spoke to my heart and said: *"All I require of you is to be my Rep"*. We are simply his hands and feet on earth.

> *"And whatsoever ye do in word or deed, do all in the name of the Lord Jesus,*
> *giving thanks to God and the Father by him."*
> Colossians 3:23:

> *"And whatsoever ye do, do it heartily, as to the Lord, and not unto men."*
> Colossians 3:17

What do people need?

Song writers Greg Nelson and Phil Mchugh are credited with the words found in the song People Need the Lord. Here are words of the song, in part, which beautifully expresses what we all need:

Everyday they pass me by
I can see it in their eyes
Empty people filled with care
Headed who knows where

On they go through private pain
Living fear to fear
Laughter hides their silent cries
Only Jesus hears

We are called to take His light
To a world where wrong seems right
What could be too great a cost
For sharing life with one who's lost?

People need the Lord, people need the Lord
At the end of broken dreams, He's the open door
People need the Lord, people need the Lord
When will we realize that we must give our lives?
For people need the Lord, people need the Lord.

RAP = Read And Pray

Sharing Jesus is a Great Privilege

Because of the Holy Spirit that dwells within you, opportunities will come as special gifts to present the Gospel to a lost person. These opportunities will be divine appointments that you do not want to miss because He knows when and where He has set the stage. All you have to do is be available and obedient. Listed below are some suggestions that will help you be prepared for one of the greatest days of your life – sharing Jesus with a lost person.

PREPARE and PRAY for opportunities and God will show you those who have a convicting spirit and are seekers of salvation. If you are *hungry* for sharing the gospel with a lost person – then your eyes will be open to the starving people all around you. God has called you to feed them the food He will provide (Remember the 5,000, See Matthew 14 and John 6).

"Blessed are they that hunger and thirst after righteousness:
for they shall be filled." Matthew 5:6

Be mindful of timing: A belligerent person or one who is under the influence of a substance is not in the right frame of mind to hear anything you might want to say. If a person is seeking an answer, this is always the right time and should be your first priority.

"But foolish and unlearned questions avoid,
knowing that they do gender strife." 2 Timothy 2:23

Recognize the difference in *knowing* about God and having personal *peace with God:* If you know a persons' lifestyle does not exhibit Christian beliefs then it is a reasonable assumption that he/she does not have an intimate relationship with God. This is 'fruit inspection' for a Christian cannot continue in sinful behavior and be in fellowship with God. It is appropriate to ask such a person - "If you died right now would you go to heaven?"

"Ye shall know them by their fruits.
Do men gather grapes of thorns, or figs of thistles?
Even so every good tree bringeth forth good fruit;
but a corrupt tree bringeth forth evil fruit." Mathew 7:16-17

Knowledge of God does not mean salvation or that a person has been redeemed by the blood of Jesus Christ. To have a personal intimate relationship with God, always involves mercy and grace found in the sacrifice, death and resurrection of God's Son, Jesus. Be courteous and kind, and above all be humble and unjudgmental.

"Judge not, that ye be not judged.
For with what judgment ye judge, ye shall be judged:" Matthew 7:1-2

RAP = Read And Pray

Let them know you care:. "No one cares how much you know until they know how much you care." I do not know who coined this statement but it was one of my momma favorite saying.

"Charity (love) never faileth:" 1 Corinthians 13:8

One thing non-Christians recognize first is the genuine love of the Christian person who befriends them because that person is 'different'. They may not know what causes the difference but they want it. Such was so with Jennifer whom we met on vacation. She told me that I was different and she wanted to know how and why? I told her. She accepted Jesus as her personal Savior that day while on her job.

Be ready to fearlessly obey:: While your testimony will not save a person, testifying of Jesus' sacrifice will. Be sensitive to opportunities to tell your story; but keep in mind it's not your story they need, so keep it brief and to the point. When the Apostle Paul gave account of his salvation story he always talked about what happened to him on the road to Damascus and when talking about himself he gave less detail but did let it be known he was a harden sinner who persecuted The Church. His emphasis was on the story of Jesus, not the story of Paul. Give your own testimony when appropriate, but remember it is not about you.

*"Then Ananias answered, Lord, I have heard by many of this man,
how much evil he hath done to thy saints at Jerusalem:
And here he hath authority from the chief priests to bind all that call on thy name.
But the Lord said unto him, Go thy way: for he is a chosen vessel unto me,
to bear my name before the Gentiles, and kings, and the children of Israel:
For I will shew him how great things he must suffer for my name's sake."* Acts 9:13-16

To the glory of God, I say, I knew a man who was speaking lies and threats against me. Under the bidding of the Holy Spirit I paid him a visit. The moment I walked in the door, his demeanor changed and we had a civil conversation. After a few years he called my husband to come to his home because he had some questions. Also by the bidding of the Holy Spirit my husband went to his home, answered his questions and led him to the Lord. He was then baptized and joined our church. When a person obeys God then God is always in control of every situation.

*"No weapon that is formed against thee shall prosper;
and every tongue that shall rise against thee in judgment thou shalt condemn.
This is the heritage of the servants of the LORD
and their righteousness is of me, saith the LORD."* Isaiah 54:17

There has been many martyrs throughout history. While we should not desire to be one we should desire to tell the old, old story of Jesus Christ and His love when and where the Holy Spirit directs.

RAP = Read And Pray

Be a Good Listener. Hear what the person is saying. Take into account their experiences and culture. While on mission to Honduras I talked to the gardener who was cutting weeds with his machete near where we were staying. One day I started a conversation with him by admiring his work. Eventually he told me there was *no way* he could be saved because he was told by another (supposedly) Christian that he couldn't. I asked why? He said: "because I have a tattoo." Many people have been given faulty information and there is usually a reason why they don't pursue God. Listen for those non-truths and then share the truth according to the Scripture. Benji was saved that day.

> *"For whosoever shall call upon the name of the Lord shall be saved."*
> Romans 10:13

Ask Questions. Find out about a person's salvation. The answer is simple, either yes or no. If they are still sitting on the fence help them to cross over on the right side. Find out if there has ever been a specific time in their life when they asked for forgiveness and trusted Jesus as their Savior. Ask them to tell you about it. If they cannot tell you about the experience itself, then guide them to a *know-so* salvation. Remember the calendar day is not the important thing. Remembering the experience is.

Follow Up. Continue to pray, visit if possible, and communicate with new believers. Notice facts. Remember things about their family, work, etc. Find something you may have in common. Relax and watch God do miracles of the heart. Be obedient to Him, led by the Holy Spirit.

Be mindful of some basic Do's and Don'ts.

RAP = Read And Pray

WITNESSING 101

Do
*Let the person tell their story. Encourage them to talk, then listen intently.
*Remove distraction.
*Pause deliberately.
*Encourage eye contact.
*Smile through your eyes.
*Nod in recognition that you understand.

Above All
*Pray silently for Holy Spirit to be in control.

Don't
*Don't condemn or ask about specific sins.
*Never give Holier-than-thou attitudes.
*Argue or criticize
*Overloud with information.
*Embarrass.
*Do not forget who you are in Christ Jesus.

Above All
Don't be afraid or get cold feet – this is not about you. It is about the gift of Eternal Life in Jesus.

The #1 reason people have difficulty believing and accepting Jesus as their LORD and Savior is because they do not believe the truth. They have been given false information. And believe it without investigation. (It's very easy to believe the lies of satan.)

All truth is found in Jesus.

Our job is to find what hinders, explain the truth, and help them receive healing and forgiveness.

RAP = Read And Pray

<u>What part do you play in witnessing for the Lord?</u>

<u>What is the Holy Spirit's job when it comes to witnessing?</u>

(Take your time to study the charts on the next two pages and look up the Scripture references. These charts will help you understand the differences in being lost compared to having peace with God; and the difference in happiness and joy.)

RAP = Read And Pray

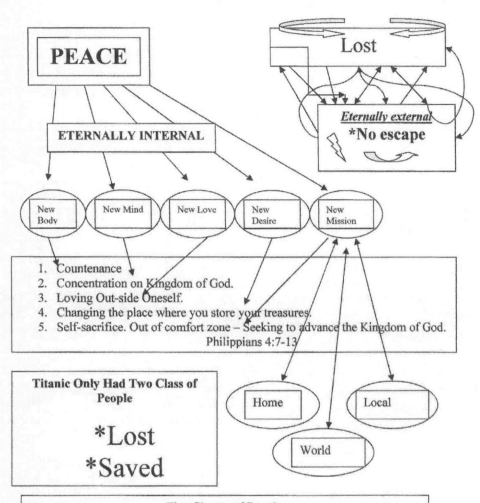

1. Countenance
2. Concentration on Kingdom of God.
3. Loving Out-side Oneself.
4. Changing the place where you store your treasures.
5. Self-sacrifice. Out of comfort zone – Seeking to advance the Kingdom of God.
Philippians 4:7-13

Titanic Only Had Two Class of People

*Lost
*Saved

Five Classes of People:
1. Out and Out Sinner – No Peace

2. Self Righteous – No Peace

3. Procrastinator – No Peace

4. Church Member of Religion – Not Salvation – No Peace

5. Redeemed. – Saved - PEACE

RAP = Read And Pray

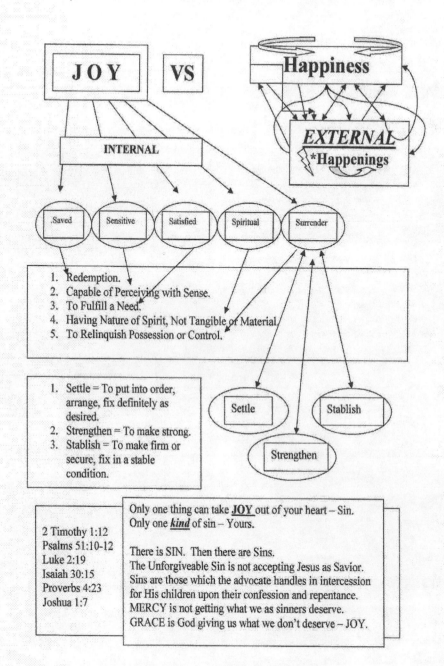

RAP = Read And Pray

Chapter 6
Grief Relief

RAP = Read And Pray

Why is this chapter necessary and important?

Why is there a chapter on grief in this study guide? Good question. Topics we have studied up unto this point concern how to start your relationship with God by way of the Cross of Calvary and reading your Bible to understanding salvation. That is where *the good life of eternal life* begins. You have been challenged to immerse yourself in personal spiritual growth by doing *your part* in the growth process. We have studied topics of:

Reading the Bible
Understanding Salvation
Prayer
Sharing Jesus

It is also important to start learning what God is about to do in order to refine you and remold you on the porter's wheel. Simply put, this is to sanctify you. And this sanctification will take the rest of the time your soul remains in your clay body on earth. During this time you will need some *grief relief*. Why? Because life happens. We are learning how to live holy in an unholy world and it can be a grievous process. However, here is the good news: You never have to go-it alone under your own strength. You know the Bible, your understand salvation, you know how to pray, and you are sharing Jesus but that doesn't mean you will not be called to suffer some along the way. Don't let it be a surprise and certainly don't let it scare you.

This section of grief relief will be helpful for you as well as for those with whom you share it with. Just because you walk through the fire personally helps you know how hot it can get and also can help you to help others know some stages are normal when they smell the smoke, walk through the fire themselves, or try to recover from the aftermath. If you live and love; you will be called to grieve at some point. And that is a fact.

Flip through these pages to see what is available but you will know when to return to them for yourself, or as tools to help friends and family members survival after tragedy. Grief is a subject that cannot be preventively taught. It's a journey but not a destination. As you continue on to chapter seven **Life As A Christian** different topics will attempt to explain the benefits of hope and trust during the process of your sanctification. This is where application takes place and faith grows.

RAP = Read And Pray

What is Grief?

The dictionary meanings for the word 'grief' is: "Grief is the anguish experienced after significant loss, usually the death of a beloved person." It goes on to say: "Grief often includes physiological distress, separation anxiety, and confusion. There may also be obsessive dwelling on the past, and apprehension about the future."

And there is more, because even dictionaries have a hard time explaining grief. In a nutshell it can be said that <u>*sorrow is anything that brings a sad tear*</u>. This is not to minimize grief because it can also appear as anything that causes immobility to function in a normal way and/or total disruption of living in a happy manner.

In order to blanket tough situations or circumstances with a verbal act of kindness, it has become a universally accepted statement to simply say "I'm sorry for your loss." This statement alone comes short of offering comfort to a person who is grieving. First, it spotlights the event as an obvious loss (to the person who is in shock or denial); and second, the loss is attached to the griever as something very personal (*their* loss). Nevertheless, let's not condemn the statement because it does at least indicate a verbal acknowledgement that an unpleasant event has happened.

Grief can happen when our expectations are not met. Disappointments in people or situations can result in stress that affects the entire person: mentally, physically, emotionally, socially, and spiritually. Humans have a need to be mentally alert, physically fit, emotionally stable, and spiritually strong. Problems come when there is not a balance in any of these. Grief also wears many hats and is dealt with in many ways.

What is Grief in Your Own Words?

RAP = Read And Pray

Grief Triggers

Grief can be triggered by so many different situations that it's impossible to individually list them all. Let's start by making a couple short lists and begin with grief involving losing a person. Check those that apply to you personally.

Causes of Personal Grief in Relationships:

- A child losing his/her parent.
- A parent losing his/her child.
- A husband losing his wife.
- A wife losing her husband.
- A sister losing her brother.
- A brother losing his sister.
- A friend losing a friend.
- A co-worker losing a trusted boss or co-worker.
- A child losing a classmate.
- A teacher losing a student.
- A policeman losing a comrade.
- A soldier losing his/her best friend.
- A loss by divorce and/or permanent separation.
- A child losing a full-time parent through divorce.
- A parent losing a full-time child because of divorce.
- Untimely death by murder.
- Untimely death by suicide.

Add others not mentioned:
_____
_____

Now look at the list again and make another check mark beside those with whom you shared spill-over grief because it has happened to someone you love. Chances are in favor that almost all events listed above have been checked.

How was your grief process different when it happened to someone else, rather than to yourself?
_____
_____

RAP = Read And Pray

Causes of Grief

Below check those that apply to you personally.

Causes of Personal Grief in Situations.

- A home loss in a tornado.
- A loss of a job.
- A loss of status.
- A child abused.
- A pet passing or mistreated.
- A lost fortune.
- A home flooded causing a start-over.
- A loss friend as result of a misunderstanding.
- A loss caused by physical pain/cancer.
- A loss of health by accident.
- A loss of another's affections.
- A loss caused by bad judgment.
- A bad hair day.
- A broken fingernail.
- A fish that got away.
- The dent on a favorite vehicle.

Add others not mentioned:
_____
_____
_____

Now look at the list again and make another check mark beside those with whom you shared spill-over grief because it has happened to someone you love – i.e. close friend.

How was your grief process different when it happened to someone else, rather than to yourself?

_____
_____
_____

Did you wonder why the last four mentioned above were included in this list? Did you think "I wish that is all I had to worry about or grieve over?"

RAP = Read And Pray

Appearance can be deceiving. A bad hair day, a broken fingernail, a fish that got away, and the dent of a favorite vehicle seem mighty insignificant to those who have experienced any of the other losses, wouldn't you agree? We should not try to line up shoulder to shoulder to see whose grief is the most severe. Jesus met people where they were and accepted everyone who received the truth. There are only two classes of people in this world. They are: Lost or Saved. Just because someone has seemingly been given a silver platter in life compared to those who have endure a horrific life, all their life – will live in the same heaven if Christians. They are not loved more or less. I've seen those who think they deserve more out of life than they have been given and I've also seen those who think they received much more than they deserved out of life.

That brings us to consider one more issue concerning causes of personal grief:

Causes of Personal Grief of Heart.

- Having been physically abused.
- Having been a physical abuser.
- Having been emotionally manipulated.
- Having been an emotional manipulator.
- Having been abandoned.
- Having abandoned.
- Having been wrongfully judged and/or condemned.
- Having been belittle or punished being innocent.
- Having punished the innocent.
- Being unable to forgive self or others.

This list could become the longest list and the toughest to answer truthfully. These things can also cause the deepest scars and most dangerous and damaging unresolved grief. Perhaps the one who broke a fingernail can check not just one, but two of the things listed above. Perhaps the one who dent a fender of his car was told as a child that he was worthless. Maybe the fish that got away brought back a memory of a drunken father who did nothing but swear and blame others for his misfortune. Could those things now be considered as "grief makers?"

*Anything that Brings Sad Tears can be interpreted as sorrow,
*Anything that brings a scar to the Soul is Grief.
*We all need Grief Relief.

RAP = Read And Pray

Acknowledging Grief

The grief caused by an event that hijackers from behind, can leave a person saying "I didn't see that coming" and is much difference than the grief of a spouse who has watched his/her loved husband/wife slowly and painfully waste away in sickness and pain. Grief wears many dresses, and no person knows how long this binding straight jacket will control daily living. In Bible days there was a designated period where those in grief sat in sackcloth and ashes while people moaned or wailed to express pain, some paid to do so, as a way for others to know something bad had happened. Today is very different. Not many people want to acknowledge or talk about grief.

When my beloved husband died after two bouts of cancer, eight years apart, I spent those eight years with grief, for him, because of what *he* had to go through. But grieving for myself didn't start until I tried to go to sleep the day of his funeral. I was indeed blindsided as to how I felt when grief covered my entire being. I now "owned" grief to the bone. It was my grief, my very personal grief. I didn't have to advertise it, because it was obvious. Well-wishers are in a great struggle to know what to do or what to say to the person grieving. So the sad thing is they often do or say nothing in fear of doing or saying the wrong thing.

The purpose of including this topic in a basic study book of Bible Reading and Prayer is simply because grief is an event(s) of life that will happened to every single person who welcomes the light of day at birth. Grief will happen. But remember this: <u>Grief is never meant to be a destination</u>. Some choose to disregard it as a 'bad day' until those bad days disable good days. At that time it may be difficult to admit disappointments, distress and depression has turned to lifelong grief. The good news is there is a place to get a prescription for *grief relief*, but it does require taking the prescription to the pharmacy. In taking a prescription to the pharmacy to be filled, acknowledgment is made that there is a problem.

For physical pain caused by none medical conditions, knowledgeable doctors are available and may be necessary for a person caught in the grief cycle that torments. There is no shame in this. Seeking help in this manner is advised and can offer help in coping with grief. As well, as Christians we are covered with good insurance and tremendous benefits that come along with salvation. These benefits are guaranteed for a lifetime and the only copay is showing up for counseling. Grief relief is available. The first step in relief is to identify the source of pain.

When my mother died when I was twenty years old, I tried to dismiss my pain and cover my grief by saying "she is in heaven" that's enough to know. After seven years of torment, I finally realized that was not enough to know. I admitted to God that I was uncontrollably grieving and blaming Him. I did not fully believe heaven was a real place. When heaven became real to me – it changed everything!

RAP = Read And Pray

When grief involves the loss of a person through death, and since people know that death is a permanency, it can be easy to think that the grief over the death is permanent as well. Even when said afterwards: "I will never get over this, it's like it happened yesterday.". Nothing is like the onset of devastating grief. It's in a time period all its own. The depth of grief felt after death of a loved one can fluctuate depending on the depth of the relationship with the person who died. After the death of a loved one whose relationship involved intimacy or lack of it and the shock subsides, two things can happen: Grief turns into either (1) Blessed grief, or (2) Regretful grief.

(1). Blessed grief is when the relationship with the person was so intimate that communication was on a daily basis and involved sharing of ideas, plans and dreams for the future. With this kind of relationship the loneliness is very real and very emotional. Everything about daily life reminds the griever in some way of the loved one who is no longer present One of two things will happen to the survivor: (a). Either a thankful heart will develop gratefulness for what was and in time will appreciate and embrace each new good thing that is still yet to come. Or, (b). The depression associated with the loss of the loved one will override trusting God that He will orchestrate the future to His divine purpose. And, He will do this faithfully for His children because His desire is to bless, support and nurture us with His love. Our part is to love God back. Healing will then come.

This is not in any way a substitute for the previous life; but, rather, it is an addition of opportunities for future happiness and good memories. The thankful heart wants to remember what was but will also make room for what can be; and, *can be* with guiltlessness. New blessings are not meant to substitute or take the place of yesterday; but on the contrary new blessings are simply that. New.

(2). Regretful grief is when the relationship with the person who died was not intimate, but should have been, and there was lack of communication with little hope that things would be better. Now, after the death there would be no hope that dreams of such will ever happen. This is the "I should have" condition of blame that has no useful purpose for in the future because the past is past. Nevertheless, we all do this to some degree in hopes of making sense out of nonsense. This condition is best diagnosed and treated with an intense dose of truth from God's Word on forgiveness and love, as well as personal counseling with a qualified Christian counselor.

RAP = Read And Pray

Both of these types of grief can result in greater understanding of the love of Jesus Christ and the pass-through can result in spiritual growth instead of extended grief. This page is for reference only because these topics go very deep and can affect all areas of life. That is why the griever should emerge into God's word for healing and claim the promises of God which can only be found in fellowship with Him. He is the only one who is promised to always fill that spot in the heart that requires intimacy and fellowship on a daily, 24-7, always on call, in case of emergency person available anytime, including the darkness of night.

When tears come and a hug is needed, grab a blanket and a Bible and cuddle with God. He is waiting.

RAP = Read And Pray

Responding to the Stages of Grief

Being a Christian does not eliminate bad things from happening to good people. But being a Christian with a loving Church family offers a source of strength that cannot be found in any other place. Sure we may say the wrong thing at the wrong time but at the core of ignorance lies a loving heart who has not yet experienced the kind of pain or torment that throw someone into the pit of despair. They understand only what they know, and they don't know what they don't know until they know what they didn't know. That statement is not meant to be cute or a tongue twister.

The person who doesn't know what it feels like to loss a baby at birth or have their home and all their belongings loss in a tornado – simply does not know how that feels. Even if they had a similar situation – it is not the same as owning a current tragedy. Immediately after the passing of a trusted loved one those left behind are the ones who are thrust into permanent earthly separation from the deceased. The loss is great and hope of ever having another hug (as was known) from the decease is gone. Without hope, life can be empty and devastating. Here lies the miracle. The Christian is never without hope of resurrection. Heaven finally becomes a real place to the grieving Christian. This comfort is only available to those who have found peace with God. A man told me once that if his (deceased) son was not in heaven, then he didn't want to go there either. This logic is tragic and faulty thinking. Perhaps you know someone who is so swallowed up in grief that all logic is gone. The best thing you can do is lead that person to the foot of the Cross of Calvary and help them understand what true love looks like.

In the process of grief there are certain natural steps in recovery. Often, really usually, there is the initial response where the first emotion is **shock**. Following shock comes a period of **panic** because part, most or all of life as-we-know-it has changed. Then **numbness** – that to me, is the partializing moments turned to hours - turned to days - turned to weeks - turned to months and so on and so on. One may say – "I don't feel like doing *nothing*." Don't nurse or pet this period of time by rallying it in. So, if you don't feel like it – start to think about it anyway. **Denial** may run alongside **numbness** for a while and there may be rocks in the way to stumble on that will make a person **angry** or **resentful.**

Anyone can google the *Five Stages of Grief* on the internet, and it will come up as:

1. **Denial**
2. **Anger**
3. **Bargaining**
4. **Depression**
5. **Acceptance**

What google doesn't tell you is how to get from one to another with the goal being # five. In the first-place acceptance means to most that "I'm ok with what happened." Never. Not with deep grief that vexes the soul. Acceptance doesn't mean one is satisfied or ok with

RAP = Read And Pray

what happened. It means what happened doesn't control every wake moment nor is it allowed to change the course of walking in fellowship with God. Many times we don't understand "why God allowed it to happen" but never should we live like bad things that happened are ordained by God. Bad things (that we interpret as "bad") can result in something unimaginatively different than expected. A kernel of corn can be buried after it has seemingly died and is seemingly useless. Then one day push up from the ground and yield a stalk that will produce hundreds or thousands of other kernels. It is resurrected.

While a missionary in Honduras I met a local woman who confessed to be a Christian but had lose all joy entitled to her. After a lengthy conversation the real problem surfaced. She had a friend who was having horrible dreams and could not sleep. In an effort to help her friend she had prayed that God allow her to "take some of the pain" on her friends behalf. Why? Because she thought she was strong enough to handle it, more so than her tormented friend. She found out otherwise. While we are taught in the Scripture to bear one another's burden – that does not mean to judge satan's power as something we can handle physically on our own merit. It is not pleasing to God for us to carry more than our own share of misery and pain. Praying such is unbiblical. No one has ever been able to stand toe to toe with satan except the One and Only Son of God. He proved that while He was on earth. If we could take on satan by ourselves then what would be the point of having Jesus come to earth in the first place? We are to walk along side and be a helper – not the solution. Only Jesus Christ can handle that job.

Being a grief sharer is making time to take time to just be there. No one has to think ahead what to say or do. Just be genuine and the Holy Spirit will guide you in ways to help the griever. This is a great benefit of being a Christian. You never have to face grief and its affects alone. If it's your turn to be the griever; then you can be sure other Christians are grieving right along with you helping in ways that are pleasing to God but may be unknown to you, however grief supporter are not the answer or the healer. Jesus Christ occupies that position. If you are the griever or the grief supporter there any many things to do in order to start the process to healing. This is the place to read and activate the book of Romans, paying attention especially to chapters 8, 12 and 13. Before continuing to the next topic stop and read them because you will find help and hope in the words. You will learn how not to conform but rather be transformed into a new being through humility and joining yourself with the support group of the Church. There is a job there where you can use your God given talents, you will rejoice with those that rejoice and weep with those that weep. You will learn that God will avenge, when necessary, and this relieves you of that responsibility so there is no need for you to try to figure it out or take matters into your own hands. There is also lots of encouragement for any stage of life you may be dealing with.

"Rejoicing in hope; patient in tribulation; continuing instant in prayer."
Romans 12:12

RAP = Read And Pray

Grief Timetable

The bakery chef may want to argue with the person who says that baking a red velvet cake is the same as baking an Italian cream cake. You say a cake is a cake! But the one in the kitchen knows different. The cakes look different, smell different and taste different. The *Red Velvet* cooks for 45 minutes on 350 degrees but the *Italian Cream* has to cook ten minutes longer on 375 degrees. The ten minutes and twenty-five degrees makes the difference when the cake is turned bottom side up on the countertop when done.

No one can tell the griever how long grief will last because only the griever knows when it is done. Just as there is vulnerability in taking a cake out of the oven before it's time; there is vulnerability in forcing oneself to act as if all is normal when all is most definitely not normal, nor expected to be ever again. A new normal has to be established.

If you haven't studied the story of Joseph's journey in life, then take time now to read Genesis chapters 35, 39-50. I will attempt to make a long story, become short. However, you must read this in the Bible to get the full scope of Joseph's incredible life journey. God's timetable of grief certainly was not the way Joseph expected his dreams to materialize and it was not ever easy. Let's look at a few points here that will be useful during your "wait and hope" phases of life.

Joseph had a dream that he would be elevated to authority and even his family would bow down to him. His older brothers became ferociously jealous of him and all but one wanted to actually kill him. Reuben objected. Events turned opposite of what Joseph dreamed and expected. His grief began. Joseph did not just go along with his brothers nor lay down in the pit, wave goodbye and take a nap. He was devastated because he was abandoned and rejected by his brothers and he knew they could hear him desperately crying out after them. His cry's landed on deaf ears. The next twenty-two years Joseph would be separated from not just these brothers but also his entire family. He had no ideal at the time that the Lord would use these hard conditions as a training ground for a greater purpose that awaited him.

After being sold to Potiphar, an officer of Pharaoh in Egypt, he was falsely accused of immorality and ended up in jail for two years. The dreamer turned into an interpreter of dreams and was delivered from jail when he revealed the meaning of Pharaoh's dreams; which event would grant him the prestigious position of being the second most powerful man in Egypt. A famine was coming and God would use this famine to bring the family back together again. This reunion would not happen because the brothers came crawling back to him asking for forgiveness, but rather because Joseph found it in his heart to forgive. Prayerfully read this event recorded in Genesis chapter forty-five paying special attention to how Joseph cried on his brothers as tears of forgiveness washed away his bitterness and he said that "God sent me before you to preserve you a posterity in the earth, and to save your lives by a great deliverance. So now it was not you that sent me hither, but God:" (Genesis 45:7-8)

RAP = Read And Pray

Those tears were not for a show; but rather necessary for release and healing salve for Joseph's soul. There were no bargaining tactics or ultimatums issued such as – "you do this then I will do that". The best way when forgiveness is needed; is to always give it freely with no strings attached. Bargaining may backfire and ultimatums usually will not turn out the way you expect, plus be very costly and sometime involve permanent separations. Never focus on the pain caused by someone because that cripples progress and it's better to focus on the healing because it is greater than the hurting. During reconciliation with a person, if the case be so that caused your grief, remember this one thing: If you are one of the lucky ones who receives an apology, don't dismiss it by saying "it's ok". Instead say – "I forgive you". This releases the guilty and sets you free as well. Let go of the past, forgive and then you will have peace in the present.

We can try to hurry God's purpose to fulfill the plan but His way is the best way. When you have days during your periods of grief that you wonder "what's the use anyway", then you stop for just a minute and think about this story of Joseph. When he revealed himself to his brothers he did not begin by reminding them what they had done to him; he revealed himself to them as "their brother". The fastest and surest way to start the healing process during grief involving injury to your soul is to let go of the past, forgive others because then and only then can one have true peace and happiness in the present as God's plan is still in the dark.

In situations where a lot of people are involved, remember God is working with people who might be just as stubborn as yourself when it comes to forgiveness as far as letting go of bitterness and resentment. God had not revealed his total plan to Joseph, yet Jospeh still went on about his life anyway. Joseph knew where his family was but his family did not know where he was. Which meant that perhaps Joseph could have taken matters into his own hands and been a tattletale to Jacob. But that was not God's way of saving the life of his father as well as all the rest of his family.

No one can tell you how long your grief with last and if they say after a year's anniversary of an event all is forgotten and well with your soul, they are misleading you. Handling your grief is a very personal thing but I can say that according to Scripture, when your focus is on God's way and God's plan, you can have patience during the wait. Don't put your hope in changed circumstances or even changed people; put your trust, hope and faith in God. He is the healer. So, ask Him for the healing. Whatever you do, don't be angry and blame Him.

What is "righteous indignation?" Indignation means anger, resentment and outrage. So how can you use the two words; righteous and indignation together? Sinful anger during grief is when we are upset to the point of blaming God. Righteous indignation is when God is upset with us because we are disappointed in Him. Simply remember the old saying, God is good and *all the time* God is good. Disrespecting Him hinders recovery and negatively affects the timetable for healing. .

RAP = Read And Pray

Dealing With Grief

As with me, you may have grown up listening to Billy Graham's messages over the radio or television and tried to hang onto his every word. Rarely or never did they show the entire crowd of hundreds of thousands of people who flooded into the arena where he was to preach. Why, it was not about the crowds, for Billy Graham it was about the person. That person being Jesus Christ.

I've walked the aisle at The Cove that houses The Billy Graham Training Center and sat in the seats on many occasions. I've read the books, listened to the tapes and not once did anything boomerang to Billy Graham. He never wanted to be considered a mighty man of stature. For him, it was – and I quote when he said: "All I am is a spectator watching God work." Humbly said.

The person who thinks fellowship with God only rewards a cup of tea occasionally, has never sat with their feet under His table. A person can practice grief in many ways, such as spilling milk, a broken fingernail, or a bad hair day. We grieve over other things such as a lost key or a lost job. If you have not ever lost any of these things then how can you know how it feels? At the moment of the lost key, plans are halted to jump in the car. All plans to get where you are going are postponed involuntarily. Same with losing a job. The key is an easier fix than losing a job. But both require an adjustment of both plans and attitudes.

For the Christian, as such you are (never forget) the process to recover starts immediately, not under your own power but by the power of Jesus Christ. The benefit for a Christian is they/we should first recognize that God has a plan, and that plan must have time to run its course. The lost key is very personal but can affect more than one person. Without it you may not be able to go to work on time or carry the kids to school.
A lost job will affect not only the unemployed but also the entire family and even the church. How the church? Because with no job there is no money to put in the offering plate. Do you think God likes that? He has a plan. (Let's assume as a Christian you know all about tithing; if not – you have missed the best of the best in blessings.) When we steal the right from God to do with His money what He wants, (by way of His Church mission) we actually rob Him.

My sister Betty who passed away in 2010 was the most stable of all ten of momma and daddy's kids. She loved life. She loved God. She loved me. She called me one morning to give me this gem of life.

"Brenda, I've been thinking about using my tithe money to help a neighbor in need, so I asked God if it was ok? You know what He told me?"

Knowing my sister had indeed heard from God, I said: "What did He tell you?"

RAP = Read And Pray

She said God answered her question by asking her a question. He said: "Why don't you give them some *of your* money?"

God has a lot of takers but fewer givers. There is an art to asking God questions and there is a responsibility in responding. That is to accept His answer of either, no, yes, wait or may even be answering by asking a rough question of His Own as happened to my sister. Dealing with personal grief or trying to help others who are in a state of grief requires some sacrifice.

At the point of being hit in the gut with a situation; we bend over in pain, and it takes a while to catch our breathe. That is a normal reaction to the action. God has you covered during the times when you can't pray for yourself – He brings you to the mind of your brothers and sisters in Christ and instructs them what to do to help you.

The grievers' mission is to come to realize that shock, panic, anger, numbness, and even denial are all a natural part of the grief process. The grief supporters' mission is to be ready to enter into a messy situation that requires being under God's umbrella during the storm.

In the book entitled "The Billy Graham Christian Worker's Handbook, that is a comprehensive counseling guide there is a section called: "Bereavement: Dealing With Grief". (Compiled by BGEA Spiritual Counseling Department. Published by Worldwide Publications, Copyright 1981 by the Billy Graham Evangelistic Association.) I do not attempt to verbatim any part of this magnificent material, but it is a great resource for church leaders as well as home libraries.

One thing most grievers will agree upon is that the road is hard and one never knowns once the rain of tears start how long the storm will last. Tears will mingle without words for no one knows the perfect thing to say. That's ok. Pre-preparation is worth its weight in gold when it comes to memorizing God's Word. In times when thinking and reasoning is absent, memorized Scripture will come like a light in a dark room. The joy of the Lord and His promises will start the healing process. As you grieve be mindful not to grieve the Holy Spirit as well. We do that by not calling on Him for help.

"And grieve not the Holy Spirit of God, whereby ye are sealed unto the day of redemption. Let all bitterness, and wrath, and anger, and clamor, and evil speaking, be put away from you, with all malice: and be ye kind one to another, tenderhearted, forgiving one another, even as God for Christ's sake hath forgiven you." Ephesians 4:30-32

"But Jesus beheld them, and said unto them,
With men this is impossible;
but with God all things are possible."
Matthew 19:26

RAP = Read And Pray

When one thinks the pain of grief is too grievous to bear, - God says otherwise.

*"I can do all things through Christ
that strengtheneth me."*
Philippians 4:13

"For with God nothing shall be impossible."
Luke 1:37

This kind of power is far more than the power of positive thinking. It is the power of God that makes what seems impossible possible.

How strong is your faith today?

Do you need to strength your faith in God?

How can a person become emotionally stable and spiritually strong?

How can your best help others during their times of sorrow?

RAP = Read And Pray

Grief Recovery

Jesus' mother bore a son whom she knew would someday die to save the world. I imagine she did not let that knowledge keep her from loving her little boy with pure joy and happiness even though she knew someday He would suffer. She learned how to enjoy the current days rather than overshadow them with dread of the future. Remember, she was the one who told the servants to do what Jesus said in providing wine (turned water into wine) for a wedding. She knew it was time. Jesus knew what it meant for Him as well. She let Him know, as His mother, it was alright, and she would be ok. She would be ok even knowing her precious baby turned man must obey His Father. And that would require unthinkable pain and suffering.

Was Mary's pain excruciating? Of course it was. Is grief excruciating? Of course it is and it cannot be avoided. Grief is part of living, and some have a whole lot more to grieve over than others. Is this fair? No. Life does not treat a person fairly. Otherwise a parent would never be called to grieve over the loss of a child, nor a child grieve over the loss of a parent.

Having spent many years in the school system there was a time when two young girls loss their mother to cancer. They were absent from school for a month while their father tried to do what a good father does for himself and his children. When the girls came back to school the youngest, age five was having trouble coping. I was given the privilege of taking care of her that on some days allowed me to just sit and rock her in a rocking chair near the school office, while she took a short nap. Did her grieve spill-over on me? Of course it did. Was this a legitimate reason to leave my other responsibilities as a good employee? It was one of the most important and rewarding things I ever did. I was a grief sharer. To some all I did was take a break and rock a child. To the child and me it was so much more.

All grievers must take breaks from it. Otherwise, grief consumes and creates more of the same. Growing up as a preacher's daughter I attended more than my share of funerals. I hated them because of the sad songs and tears. Since the onset of Covid 19 in early 2020 there has been a shift in the process of funerals. People were isolated at home and separated from their loved ones in hospitals. There were no visits and very little contact with anyone outside ones household. Social activities ceased, funerals were delayed or cancelled all together that left the households alone during some of the most difficult days they would ever experience. Churches were closed as well. It was a very different difficult time. Most everyone lost someone important to them as family members or friends. And the thing was, everyone in the world suddenly had to adjust to a new normal in daily life. While the new normal brought hardships it also brought some relief to others. The pandemic created time to do nothing or at least slow the rat race pace of life. What I have witnessed since that time is a change in the old familiar funeral. Up sprang services called "Celebration of Life" or "Memorials".

In the south where I live, front porch socials that had always been a part of neighborhood pleasure became yelling at one another from the car window or sitting in the driveway

RAP = Read And Pray

together looking but not touching. Hugging grandma and grandpa was discouraged in order to 'protect' them. Visiting anyone in the hospitals and nursing homes was strictly forbidden. The lonely got lonelier. Many profound and wise counseling sessions took place on front porches and around a crowded kitchen table on Sundays after church. Kids running outside to play in the rain, with only their imaginations, helped wash away dirt but more importantly it also washed away many scars.

People were not able to make funeral arrangements as normal because there was a backlog of service providers More people began to choose cremation and wait up to a year for any public acknowledgement of death. While there was around 687 million cases of Covid 19 reported worldwide, some statistics pointed to over 6.8 million deaths worldwide, with the United States recording 1.1 million of these deaths. Some statistics show Alabama as the 18th highest in the nation reporting over 100,000 deaths from March 2020 - March 2023. One of these statistical charts pointed to the most deaths occurring in the fall of 2021..

While I cannot endorse these statistics as verifiable, I do know for a fact that I personally loss upward of forty close friends during these two years. Several directly from covid, including my mission mother as well as her son and her daughter. I could not grieve over her remains or with her family and friends. But I did stand in front of my memory mirror and weep.

Does it still hurt? Of course. But I choose to rejoice over the good memories and celebrate the heaven bound reunion of those who were saved by grace. Knowing heaven is a real place and destination is where all comfort lies. I will say that again, - heaven is a real place!

We were scheduled to be in Maui a week after the fire that devastated the Island in 2023. The fire affected our plans and schedule, but it totally devastated the inhabitants. We were just going to visit, but this was home to others. This event was shared by a lot of people in a lot of different ways because it picked up normality and smashed it to smithereens.

Recovery after the onset of grief can be slow and painful for some while it may only be momentarily uncomfortable for others, depending on their investment in the circumstances. When my mother passed away when I was only twenty years old, I felt angry at the entire world, and God because He was the only one who could have prevented this tragedy. The sun was still coming up every day as usual and people were still going their merry little way when my world had suddenly stopped. Everything as I ever knew it was suddenly gone forever. The person whom I knew always prayed for me was gone. The pedestal I put her on tumbled. And I felt no other person had ever felt the torment I was feeling. I could not see life pass that moment. How can someone come out of such a pit of despair and/or faulty thinking? One Way. The Way. Seven years later, I accepted The Way, The Truth and The Life and allowed *Him* on the pedestal of my heart.

RAP = Read And Pray

Is grief recovery A B C? No, sometimes it makes no sense at all, and we have no clue as to where to start or what to do. It is one day at a time – walking in Faith.

Have you experience personal grief during a pandemic such as Covid 19?

Does it help to know others were also grieving because of the same event?

List ways you coped during personal sorrow:

How did you help others cope?

Has your faith in God been strengthen since that time? Explain:

What are some pitfalls of living in the "what if" state of mind?

How powerful are Scripture promises concerning heaven?

Are you convinced heaven is a real place? Why or why not?

RAP = Read And Pray

Grief as a Badge of Honor

Grief should never be a person's claim to fame. It's easy to unconsciously linger in grief's shadow because of thinking there is a legitimate right to be there. It either was deserved or else it was a faulty sentence that condemned the innocent. The event overshadows all that was once good and right. Had this been a legitimate place to dwell then God would have left Jesus in the tomb forfeiting our right to Salvation. Salvation is not solely about the death of Christ Jesus – it is about His Resurrection. Jesus did not come out of the grave all un-done and a bloody mess. He came out glowing as the noon day sun. While Jesus' death is the door to peace with God; Resurrection is where the door hangs. Salvation and peace with God hinges on Jesus' resurrection. Because of this, *The Door* opens to those who are saved and is closed to those who reject Christ. Death is not Jesus' badge of honor – His resurrection is.

The event that started the grief process is not as important as what happens as a result. For the Christian that often is a total reliance on God to see us through the days that follow. We become the helpless child who desperately needs a loving father. We need protected and loved and God is faithful to do both plus be our provider as well. We are still just as protected, loved and provided for as we were the day before the onset of grief. Did Jesus wear His death as a badge of honor? No! He wears His resurrection in honor to His Father.

Jesus fully trusted God to take care of all the details after Jesus earthly death. His body before His resurrection was useless to God's purpose. But, after Jesus' resurrection death was forever defeated and the sting of death annihilated. His death at Calvary was the means to the purpose. Likewise sometimes the grief we are called to bear is the means to a greater purpose not yet seen or realized. Therefore we must quit focusing on the event and instead trust God with the purpose.

This kind of purpose of being puts whatever event got us there as a shadow, not a highlight or badge to wear. If brokenness made a person whole; then bless the whole, not the pieces. Just as some form of grief is guaranteed, the healing from it is the reward as the pain that consumes is consumed. In other words that that destroys is destroyed. Let go of it.

Keeping this truth in the forefront of everyday existence yields truthful thinking rather than faulty thinking and the badge of grief can be taken off. Honor comes from accomplishment; not defeat so in Christ Jesus we have the victory!

> *"But thanks be to God, which giveth us the victory through our Lord Jesus Christ. Therefore, my beloved brethren, be ye steadfast, unmovable, always abounding in the work of the Lord, forasmuch as ye know that your labor is not in vain in the Lord."*
> 1 Corinthians 15:57-58

RAP = Read And Pray

Grief that Separates

Grief can separate oneself from other things, places or people for a time and a reason. The griever must remember that grief is a temporary pass-through, not the destination. Just as grief is for a season it is not a permanent portrait or definition.

The sadness of grief wants to unload its suitcase and make itself at home. And the glue of idleness is a quick adhesive There is a proverb that refers to idleness as the place where the devil sets up shop. An idle mind and idle hands are not pleasing to God and will not bring a person out of the pit of despair. The deceiver (satan) will take advantage of an unfocused mind. It is vitally important to reunite with familiar faces who will understand and remind the griever of basic important facts concerning God's faithfulness and presence. While these well-wishers may not always be appreciated or welcomed, don't dismiss them.

Jesus knew grief and cried to the point of weeping. Not just crying – but weeping. There is nothing wrong with tears. But what happened after Jesus wept? He got up. He put his feet to the ground and He walked toward the source of grief. He was about to resurrect someone. In this case Jesus resurrected Lazarus so can He *resurrect the griever* from grief. God offers healing of all kinds and nature and I'm sure He still has some unused or rejected miracles ready for those who will ask for them. We have not because we ask not and sometimes we ask for less than what His divine purpose may be.

It is also worthy to note that God also likes for us to just be still and know that He is God and He is in control. That's comfort enough for a hurting heart. That kind of faith is called *trust*. Whatever you do in times of trouble don't separate yourself from others who love you and especially don't separate yourself from God. Separation makes it easy to withdraw from life and all it's pleasures. A few days of separation for reflection sake is healthy, but extended separation and withdrawal from things previously enjoyed is a warning sign that healing is hampered. Even though there will be times of loneliness we must remind ourselves that we are never really alone. Then, we begin to *feel* again and see hope for the future.

"I will not leave you comfortless: I will come to you. Yet a little while, and the world seeth me no more; but ye see me: because I live, ye shall live also. At that day ye shall know that I am in my Father, and ye in me, and I in you. He that hath my commandments, and keepeth them, he it is that loveth me: and he that loveth me shall be loved of my Father, and I will love him and will manifest myself to him."
John 14:18-21

RAP = Read And Pray

Grief Retaliation

The injured wants retaliation and wants it quick. That is not God's way. He instructs us to let Him handle it. "Vengeance is mine, I will repay." Saith our Lord. Assuming a person is a Christian and has read his/her Bible, is attached to a body of believers in a Bible believing congregation and knows how to pray; these things make for victory in the life of a person in grief. Otherwise, where does the injured person go for support? Family members and/or friends are ready to offer advice. There is one thing missing that these well-wishers cannot give. That is peace. No one can have peace of the soul without first having peace with God.

It is hard enough for the Christian to have peace during stress, discouragement, depression and confusion. So what makes a Christian think that the unsaved should respond to stressful situations as if they have the help of the Holy Spirit? We have the ever-ready helper to call upon day and night and we still mess up from time to time. If one has an unsaved friend who is in the midst of despair, they need a Christian friend more than ever. That is why we need knowledge, wisdom and preparation not just to survive grief ourselves' but also to know how to help others who may be ready to do something they shouldn't in attempt to rectify a bad situation.

In the microwaveable, technical, instant gratification society we live in, what used to take weeks or months to accomplish now is available momentarily. A person can have breakfast on the East Coast and then go to bed watching the sun go down on the Golden Gate Bridge in California. Yet, we cannot walk a straight line or have time to Read and Pray. Is it any wonder that confusion clouds the mind? Time is wasted trying to organize too many mindless activities that only guaranteed returning chaos. Trying to settle thoughts of retaliation by flooding social media does not work by gathering "likes" and having 10,000 people on your side of perceived justice. Airing dirty laundry only stinks up everything else. For the person who is really serious about receiving healing, it may include throwing the rally-of-support microwave out and take time to think though the situation while sitting on a peaceful porch swing, then pray and run to the Scripture to know how to do the next 'right' thing that leads to healing.

Life outside Jesus Christ is a vicious cycle, leading to exhaustion, confusion and fear. Jesus knew what would happen in the next two thousand years following His return to be with His Father. Nothing comes as a shock to God and He never has to figure out what to do. His plan has been in place since He divided the seas and hung the sun. Jesus told us before He moved back to heaven that He would come again – in like manner. That is not a possibility – it is as true as the nose on your face. He is coming again, and we are running out of time to help our friends and family see the truth of God's Word. This is the purpose of life. This is the Christian's mission.

How does this have anything to do with the process of grief? Christians forget sometimes that as a Child of God we have been gifted with the person of counsel and guidance found

RAP = Read And Pray

in the Holy Spirit. He should be the One to hear your woos before you try to find solace in any other way. Learning to receive His counsel of wisdom and truth is the best defense against self-pity. The Christian walks by faith and not sight and is ever ready to give an account of the fact and how it happened.

The person ready to take matters in their own hands after a tragedy need to have someone who knows how to respond with wisdom, in a peaceful manner, without judgment, partiality or hypocrisy. I must ask myself and you must ask yourself – "as Christians are we ready to be that person?" Are we capable of such? We have not because we ask not and live way beneath the privileges available to us through Jesus Christ.

Let's not forget that the entire time we live on earth from the point of salvation that we are being sanctified by God to live our best life and to help others live their best life as well. Perhaps we need to disconnect from people and things that bring us down with negative attitudes and/or visions of doom and gloom.

The great news about being sanctified is that it allow a person to breathe. We do not have to "do it all" - we just have to do the-next-right-thing. What can be more wonderful than a break from trying under our own power to solve a problem? If a particular situation still has a stronghold on your mind; then, literally write it down, put it through a shredder and with faith intact take the first step to walk away from it.

Since God is more interested in us "being" rather than anything we might "do" He will honor all efforts of trusting Him with the 'doing' part. Just be His Rep in all situations and He will amaze you at what He will do to handle stressful situation without your help. It is sometimes easy to forget that God is the Father, and we are the child. He does not have to explain to you what He intends to do. He just wants you to trust Him and He will take care of it.

Everyone wants justice but needs mercy more. When Jesus Christ was hanging on the Cross at Calvary. Wasn't He in a bitter-sweet moment? (Bitter for Him, but the outcome was sweet for us.) He didn't appreciated the unfairness when He was suffering but He let it run its course. He was at a moment so alone on Calvary that He yelled out -"My God! Why have you forsaken me?" (Mark 15:34) Yet He did not seek retaliation. To do so would have voided the plan of salvation. He had purpose and was faithful to that purpose.

"God is our refuge and strength, A very present help in trouble." Psalm 46:1

*"Be still and know that I am God: I will be exalted among the heathen,
I will be exalted in the earth."*
Psalm 46:10

RAP = Read And Pray

Soul Care in Grief Relief

The Holy Spirit is in charge of your soul-care. Your soul is in good hands. Later we will talk in depth about soul-care through sanctification, which is a necessary component to survival. Jesus Christ as the Son of God is the only person who ever walked on this earth who did not need to be sanctified. He was more than saintly and more than a Saint, He was God in the flesh. The mission He accomplished while on earth was to defeat death and give life to our eternal Soul. He accomplished His mission without any flaw. This was a task that no other being could qualify for or ever accomplished. We can do things we cannot do because of the One who dwells within us.

Corrie Ten Boom was a prisoner during the holocaust. As a Christian she could live a happy life following the torment because of her forgiving heart. She was forgiven of her sins and thereby she could forgive other even if they never asked for forgiveness. Well, one day a guard from the prison came to her and asked for her forgiveness. When she saw his face, her mind said 'no – not you.' Then she prayed and asked God to love Him through her because she didn't have the power to do so. And He did. She felt love for this man's soul through Jesus who makes all things possible.

On one particular mission trip to Honduras a beautiful little girl came through our clinic with her mother. Her eyes captured me. I played with her, talked to her and loved on her. Later that day I had a walk-through in a dump where people were actually living. I was not prepared to see this precious child playing in the trash where she called home. It broke my heart. Coming back into camp I saw my *Misson Mother* sitting in a chair under a shade tree. I ran to her, fell at her feet, put my head in her lap and cried like a baby.

She lifted my head and asked me if I had been to this particular place. I said, "yes". She allowed me cry than among the things she told me, I remember only one thing.

She said: "Brenda, you come and do good. You see this, you see that. Then you go home. There will always be places like you just saw, you go, and they stay here. The most important thing you can leave with them, is to share Jesus."

That started my missionary journey. It no longer was about me or even about the people who needed help desperately – my mission became about Jesus. I started looking outside myself and what did I see? The Way, The Truth and The Life. I wanted the glow He put in my heart to shine on my face. That is what attracts people when they see the evidence that you have had an encounter with Jesus. Plain and simply.

My Mission Mother lost one son and one daughter to Covid in 2021. After she cared for them while they were sick, she also died of covid on her birthday, December 21, 2021.

RAP = Read And Pray

> *"Now when they saw the boldness of Peter and John,
> and perceived that they were unlearned and ignorant men,
> they marveled; and they took knowledge of them,
> that they had been with Jesus."*
> *Acts 4:13*

I have not forgotten for a second that we are currently talking about grief and the devastation that can follow. But listen to me – Grief should never own you (If, you are a Christian). It will run its course, absolutely, and it must, but don't let it sit in your easy chair with every day filled only with the dread the night.

It's easier to look down than it is to look up. Lift our head and look up to God's power within you. Focus on that power rather than personal weakness..

> *"Now unto Him that is able
> to do exceeding abundantly above
> all that we ask or think,
> according to the power that worketh in us,
> unto Him be glory in the church by Jesus Christ
> throughout all ages, world without end. Amen"*
> *Ephesians 3:20*

RAP = Read And Pray

Joy During Grief

Can there be times of joy during grief? Absolutely – no doubt about it. There is a way of 'feeling better and even joyful,' without feeling guilt. It is simply allowing Jesus Christ on your pedestal; one day at a time acknowledge healing in the same way grief is acknowledged. The Christian has the option to acknowledge that it is impossible to be outside the scope of God's protection and love. Amidst trials the birds are singing. And those birds begin singing while dawn is still hidden in the darkness. They trust dawn is coming because they can feel it rather than see it. They have an inborn knowledge that their Creator will be faithful to cause the sun to come up every morning. Rain or shine, the sun knows what to do.

After my husband passed away I wondered if I was going to have another seven years of grief to the same extent as to when my mother died. I had the privilege of hearing my husband say to me what lot of people who have lost spouses wish they had heard. In one of our many conversations during the last three months of his life, he told me – "you will need to get out and do things and don't you dare feel guilty." I took it to mean that he wanted me to go shopping with my daughter that week. However, as I started seeing the sunsets as a beautiful moment instead of a telegram to darkness, I began to understand his wisdom.

The wonderful presence of The Holy Spirit is always available to guide people through life. No event is a surprise to God and there is no darkness on His streets. The Christian's part is to listen and obey. That is enough and all He requires. We are God's dependent. That means He is responsible for our day-to-day needs. As such He is already making provisions for us before we even know there is a need.

There are certain things, basically, that we have learned from each other already since being a Christian and we also have Jesus' example as to how He handled grief in His own life. Did He grieve over leaving his earthly family behind in order to start His intended ministry on earth? Of course He did or else He would not have went back home with Mary and Joseph when he was twelve years old and stay there until He was thirty years old. He walked the road toward Calvary, joyfully. He loved His family, but He loved His Father most. Yet, no one has ever or will ever grieve more than Jesus Christ unless it was His Father who had to look away while His Son had my sins upon His back. God knows what grief feels like, and so does Jesus.

"Bear ye one another's burdens,
and so fulfil the law of Christ."
Galatians 6:2

RAP = Read And Pray

The shapes below can represent times during grief that may cause sudden emotional changes. For instance, the first shape may be a time when you did not know which way to turn, the second shape represent a decision to look up for help and the third shape represents a period of deep thought. Take a little time to ponder on each shape and figure out where you stand today and choose which shape represents where you need to go next for your mental, emotional and spiritual well-being.

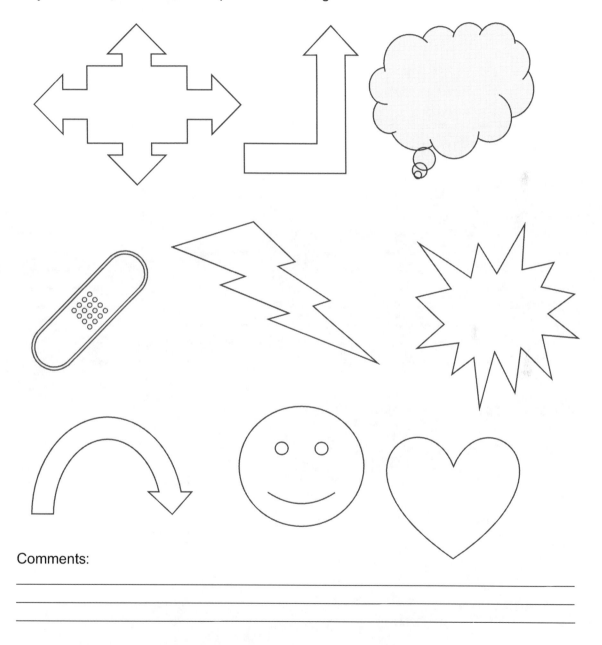

Comments:
_____
_____
_____

RAP = Read And Pray

Look up and write out Romans 8:35-39 in the space provided below:

_____
_____
_____
_____
_____
_____
_____
_____
_____
_____
_____
_____
_____
_____
_____
_____
_____
_____
_____
_____

Draw an example below as to how this makes you feel:

RAP = Read And Pray

*"Blessed are the merciful: for they shall obtain mercy.
Blessed are the pure in heart: for they shall see God.
Blessed are the peacemakers: for they shall be called
the children of God.
Blessed are they that are persecuted for righteousness sake:
for theirs is the kingdom of heaven.
Blessed are ye when men shall revile you, and persecute you,
and shall say all manner of evil against you falsely, for my sake.
Rejoice, and be exceedingly glad:
for great is your reward in heaven:
for so persecuted they the prophets that were before you."
Matthew 5:7-12*

RAP = Read And Pray

Ponder Points

- Jesus was born. He couldn't have just been Created at that time because He already was. Thus, He started His life on earth – the same way we do; with one exception. He was the giver of souls – not the taker of one.
- Jesus lived within a family. He had One mother and One Father, plus a step-dad. He knows what it is like to grow up secure in His Father and mother's love and also know about being a part of a blended family.
- Jesus enjoyed being a part of that family, but His Father came first, as is proven by "Him being about His Father's business" teaching in the Temple, when He was twelve years old.
- The human Jesus had to make the decision when He was thirty years old to continue with His earthly family life or turn water into wine at the encouragement of His mother.
- He willingly started His ministry and knew in just three short years His Father's divine will would be for Him to feel the sting of death to His human body. He yielded to it without resistance.
- His final mission was to return to the Glorified state He was in before taking on a human form.

"Father, the hour is come; glorify thy Son,
that they Son also may glorify thee:
As thou hast given Him power over all flesh,
that He should give eternal life to as many as thou hast given Him.
And this is life eternal, that they might know thee
the only true God, and Jesus Christ, whom thou hast sent.
I have glorified thee on the earth:
I have finished the work that thou gavest me to do.
And now, O Father, glorify thou me
with thine own self with the glory that
I had with thee before the world was."
John 17:1-4

RAP = Read And Pray

Healing Guides

* Ask God to heal you.

*Immerse yourself in Bible reading and Prayer. (RAP)

*Think of God's promises.

* There is no need to apologize for your grief. It is an emotion created by God.

* Share grief with others. God's church and His Family of believers wait to help.

* Ask God to help you find purpose and meaning again.

* Everyday enjoy His World. Start by raising a window, sitting in the sun, listening to the birds sing, think on God's ever-present love, and listen to Christian music.

* Feed on the promises of God.

* Even in the midst of your own grief, reach out to offer a hand to others who need help in some way. Show sympathy and offer comfort to others.

*Be faithful. Go to Church, even when your heart is not into it.

* Praise God that on earth all things will dissolve, but the love found in Jesus Christ is strong and eternal.

*As God raised Adam from the dust of the earth, He can heal you of your grief – no matter the cause or costs.

> *"Trust in the LORD with all thine heart;*
> *And lean not unto thine own understanding.*
> *In all thy ways acknowledge Him,*
> *and He shall direct thy paths."*
> *Proverbs 3:5-6*

RAP = Read And Pray

Your Story

Use the next several pages to log your story, either in words or draw a graph with the ups and downs of your life since your birth to present. Be creative. If you currently fall below the normal level (for whatever normal your life may be) then the possibility is one of many reasons. The most severe is being out of fellowship with God. That is the root of depression, extended grief, bitterness and resentment. Those who walk close to God have great support where God will heave you up in His arms for a peaceful night's sleep or strength to get through your day. See Him by *Reading and Praying* (RAP) and allowing others to walk beside you in this situation/ circumstance. Join Him where they are – in a good Bible Believing, Bible Preaching Church.

Samples of graphs if you struggle with written words:

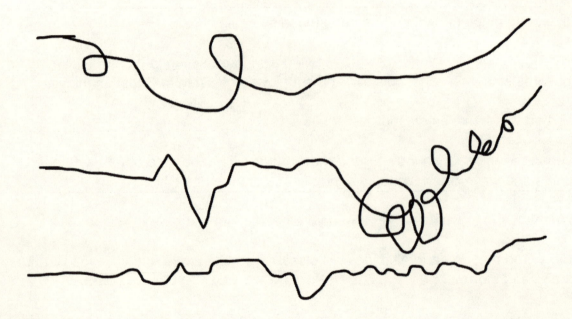

DRAW YOUR LIFE-LINE BELOW:

RAP = Read And Pray

Draw a picture of where you were when you invited Jesus into your heart and got saved:

Draw a picture of where you were in your happiest moment:

Describe your life now in one sentence:

Describe your life when you were at you lowest in one sentence:

Describe your life then when you were at your most peace in one sentence.

What changed from your lowest moment to your highest moment?

Where are you in your walk with God right now?

RAP = Read And Pray

Write out -Your Story

Write your story in your own way, take your time, you may need to come back to these pages every day until you are satisfied it is about you – not any other person. Just you. If you feel more comfortable not recording your life on these pages; then grab some paper and pencil, write it, keep it, burn it, etc. just write it out, and think of ways to get better, get healed, or stay on your settled joy of growing in your relationship and fellowship with God, Jesus Christ, and The Holy Spirit.

_____

Date:_____

RAP = Read And Pray

Chapter 7
Life As A Christian

Reconciliation Through Regeneration

Justification

Sanctification

Glorification

RAP = Read And Pray

Four Important Words in the Christian Walk

Reconciliation I need it.
(You & Me lost)
Justification He did it.
(You & Me saved)
Sanctification He is doing it.
(You & Me learning to live holy in an unholy world)
Glorification He will do it.
(You & Me living holy in a holy world – heaven)

*God gifted you a Holy Soul in your mother's womb.
He will judge that soul at your death.
Only the Holy sanctified Soul can be returned to God.*

RAP = Read And Pray

Spiritual Growth

The first gift God gives a person is their individual soul which cannot be duplicated, destroyed cloned or misplaced.

In order for spiritual growth to begin a person must first understand the nature of the soul. Simply put, everyone's soul dwells in a state of either eternal life or eternal death. That state of being is determined during the time the soul is in the earthly body. Therefore in order for a person to grow spiritually, they must be eternally alive in Christ Jesus.

This section focuses on the growth process in light of understanding where a person *was* (separated from God), what happened in the <u>Reconciliation</u> (finding peace with God), then proceed to the different in <u>Justification,</u> <u>Sanctification</u> and <u>Glorification.</u> These four things need to be understood in the beginning of a person's relationship with God and continue to be a focus throughout life. Understanding them will be invaluable to maturity of a Christian and be instrumental in developing an intimate relationship with our Creator.

There is no bigger blessing than for a person to be redeemed by reconciliation with God Almighty. All of life before this point is vanity.

The first day of Christianity is like going to a bowling alley and holding a bowling ball in one's hand for the very first time. You've entered a new arena. You do not know the rules and you need instructions on how to hold the heavy ball, where to stand on the lane, and how to knock down the bowling pens that appear to be far away. The pins at the end of the alley stand still and won't move without some outside force. However, you are the one who must move and maneuver your strategy in trying to get all the pens to fall at the same time. After you throw the first ball, that went straight to the gutter, you feel this is a ginormous impossible task that is way more difficult than you thought. I mean how hard can it be to knock those white pens silly?

After many attempts to do the impossible, your idea is just to forget the rules, walk down that long aisle and just crazily kick the suckers down yourself. Who cares about the rules anyway? When that didn't work, maybe you asked an expert to show you how it was done. So they chose the right ball with the weight and size finger holes to fit their own hand. They always take a stance and look at the pens (rather than the ball), get the exact alignment and release the ball at just the right time. The ball makes a thump and starts rolling all on its own. When the ball hits its target, the pens explode against each another. When all of them fall, then that is referred to that as "a strike!" And everyone yells and some people may jump out of their seats in excitement.

The secret of bowling is to have the right ball, know where to stand and consciously focus on nothing but the target before you release the ball. As in life we may not always get a yelp of encouragement because getting a strike is not easy, but you must focus on the target and keep trying your best. Practice, experience and learning from mistakes is a good philosophy in life as well as in learning to bowl. So is Christianity. One focuses on the target – not the obstacles.

My grandson, Christian, serves our country as a member of the United State Army. He grew up on a farm and learned how to drive machinery of all kinds. He could back up a trailer hocked to a truck with precision timing and placement. He also learned from his father the correct use and handling of different weapons. These two skills have come in handy as he serves in the military. He has become a valuable asset, using the talents and gifts God has given him. And, in the process fulfilling a great need in that others have not been trained.

The importance of keeping one's eyes on the target can also be seen in the game of basketball. We enjoy seeing players who make what seem to be impossible shots. Sometimes the ball seemingly goes through the net without even touching the woven strings. Sometimes it goes round and round the basket before falling into the net and sometimes the ball just flies from half court and thumps into the basket that accomplishes what appears to be an impossibility. It is all about focusing on the target and not what is in between.

As a Christian, God chose us, and we chose Jesus. That puts power into our hands as well. The secret to being a successful Christian, as a servant to God,
is simply to stay focused. We must always identify the target before we shoot at anything. We must have the right weapon, (the Holy Spirit); we must realize the power in that weapon (miraculous deliverance); and we must always aim at the target and not each other.

There is great power within the Christian. But we must learn first and foremost that it is not about us. Christian growth is always about the one who dwells within us. That being the Holy Spirit. He gives the guidance and strength in spiritual growth and we are just the vehicle, tool, object, or conduit in which God works. A tool in His toolbox. A member on the team and a player on the court. The star is Jesus.

RAP = Read And Pray

If you are a hammer, then be the best hammer possible. Do the job for that only a hammer is qualified. If you are a lawn mower, then get out there and cut some grass. If you are a faucet, then open up and give someone a drink of living water. Tell your own story and don't be tempted to covet other tools. Be the best *you*, and that is enough.

In The Scriptures of God's Holy word you will find the answers to all life's situations. God covered it all when He inspired Holy men to pen His Word. God loved first and

the Bible teaches us how to love Him back. It starts with a desire for reconciliation caused by being separated from God because of sin. Sin cannot live in the presence of God, so we must have a desire to get rid of any and all sin within our being. We need to be reconciled with God because He never stops loving us. We are the guilty ones who caused the separation. So at His bidding, we must respond and be reconciled with Him.

WHAT DOES RECONCILATION MEAN TO YOU?

_____
_____
_____
_____
_____
_____
_____
_____
_____
_____

How has forgiving and being forgiven affected your life?

RAP = Read And Pray

Reconciliation Through Regeneration

Reconciled relationships are a blessing from God,
with the greatest blessing being a restored relationship with Him.

Read Luke 15:11-32 concerning the prodigal (wasteful and reckless) son. Read Matthew 5:23-24; Matthew 6:14-15, 2 Cor.5:18-19, and Romans 5:1-8. Then apply them to the Six Points below. Looking up and writing out these Scriptures on the next page will help you retain them to memory.

These Scripture illustrates God's attitude toward those who need forgiveness and Jesus' demand for forgiveness. In all things the Christian's responsibility is to follow Jesus and walk according to God's Holiness. While on earth Christians live in a world of full of sin; but the Christian is of a different sort, reconciled and filled with enough power to live in a world of sin without taking part in it.

Read Genesis 33:1-15 for the following six points then describe in the space provided how they apply to you in everyday life.

First: Reconciliation is worth seeking.

Second: Seeking reconciliation involves taking risks and exhibiting humility.

Third: Reconciliation may take time to be completed.

Fourth: God accomplishes ultimate reconciliation on His own free will, after we come to Him in our own free will. He gave us right to receive this reconciliation through Jesus' death on the Cross. We all have offended God by our sins. God sent His Son to show His love and therein He paid the total price for reconciliation. Through faith in Christ Jesus, we stand reconciled with God making it possible to be reconciled with others.

Fifth: God calls us to desire and be ready to reconcile with one another.

Sixth: It is part of God's divine plan for the Christian to grow spiritually during our day-by-day journey through life. One day at a time.

Question: When, where and how have you reconciled with another person since becoming a Christian?

RAP = Read And Pray

In your own words describe how each of the words below relate to *Faith in the saving grace of Jesus Christ.* **Look up Scripture concerning each.**

Rejected: Unwanted =

Recognized: Identified =

Respond: Answer =

Relationship: Connection =

Reconciled: Settlement =

Regenerated: Rebirth =

Restored: Give Back =

Received: Accepted =

Reinforced: Strengthen =

Rejuvenated: Invigorated =

RAP = Read And Pray

Forgiveness is not a Suggestion

If you have been forgiven – then you **must** grant forgiveness.

*" Once a person is born again, he is saved from **<u>the penalty of sin</u>** (Rom.8:1; Eph.2:5,8), **<u>the power of sin</u>** (Rom.6:11-14, and will ultimately be saved from **<u>the presence of sin</u>** when God takes him to heaven and gives him a new body like the body of Jesus (Phil.3:20-21). This truth is related to the three phases of salvation: justification, sanctification, and glorification."*
(Dr. Steven R. Cook posted 11-24-2013.)

In a nutshell, (A). At the point of salvation we are forgiven, can forgive, and sealed forever by Jesus' sacrifice to eternal life. We start anew as a born-again creature ready to take on the world. This is what *JUSTIFICATION* Through *REGENERATION* looks like. (B) From that day forward throughout all the days of our lives we are being sanctified, purified & concentrated. Meaning you and I are given the power to live holy in an unholy world. That is what *SANCTIFICATION* looks like. (C). Then at life's end we will be glorified. Forever in the presence of Jesus and separated from sin. This is what *GLORIFICATION* looks like.

Salvation is one act of God. Only one act is needed, - that is to be saved! However, it is important for us to know what follows the act of salvation. That is when the work of the Holy Spirit begins. We were all born with one soul, which is all we need because that soul can never die. However; that soul will be scarred by sin because we are sinners by nature. The first part of life is pureness – in the form of a tiny baby – there is total holiness. As that soul grows to the age of accountability it knows no sin. But look out – sin is on the way because we are born into a world of sin and with a selfish sinful nature. During this period, the journey toward knowing our maker – our true creator- flows in the soul with many questions as to how to reunite with our creator. Unsettled in our heart our soul hunts for reconciliation. This happens in our new birth by being JUSTIFIED in God's eyes. JUSTFICATION is the first phase. Immediately after that Sanctification begins.

This phase, sanctification, lasts a lifetime. We are constantly being sanctified because we are dwelling in God's grace. This is why we will spend the most time studying the work of Sanctification.

There has only been One person who did not have to pass through the phase of being sanctified during his walk to heaven. That was, of course, Jesus Christ. He was in heaven first; came here to earth for 33 years – living totally Sanctified during that time. He never sinned – never ever tasted sin, until He got to the Cross of Calvary and willingly took the punishment for sin while being sinless. It was at that point His blood poured out of Him, as payment for sin that He did not commit. If anyone knows how bad sin hurts – it is JESUS.

RAP = Read And Pray

Jesus is the only person ever born into humanity who did not need sanctifying. He was justified when He came to earth and stay justified in Himself as the Son of God. He never lost His Sainthood to sin. He asked His Father to Glorify His Son – that God did through Jesus' resurrection and ascension.

Perhaps some followers of Jesus hid in the bushes during the beatings and mocking of Jesus and perhaps they even walked across His blood on the street. They were not strangers to the torment of a person who was crucified. It was always a public display of humiliation and suffering. They were not blind to the process.

His disciples didn't recognize Him when He first appeared to them – resurrected. The reason they didn't recognize Him was the last time they saw him; he was a bloody mess of a man – but now *He wasn't*. They thought that to be impossible. They might in their confused state of being thought that if miraculously Jesus had survived, He no doubt would have been a pitiful bloody, disfigured man who bore evidence of a horribly mercilessly crucifixion. He would have been left unable to walk or talk. They might have expected to see Him as He was at the point of death, but – not as He was. He was calm, polite, loving, and considerate to them and did not try to shame them because of their disloyalty. He was in His glorified body, ready to visibly ascend into heaven. There was no chance whatsoever that this world could hold Jesus. He had risen from death to the body formed in Mary's womb to return to His Father from whence He came, Glorified and Holy.

So, will it be when life is finished with us here on earth? We will have a living body for a living soul, fit for eternity and be in heaven instantly with our Lord and Savior Jesus Christ..

Meditate of this truth and then take time to use the space below to draw Jesus' life. From heaven to earth – to the Cross of Calvary and to heaven again. Let it sink into your heart – such Love!

RAP = Read And Pray

"But of Him are ye in Christ Jesus, who of God is made unto us wisdom, and righteousness, and **Sanctification**, and redemption:"
I Corinthians 1:30

Jesus
"Who shall change our vile body, that it may be fashioned like unto his **Glorious** body," Phil. 3:21a

Jesus was..."delivered for our offences and was raised again for our **Justification**!"

The Way,
The Truth,
The Life!

Who can be justified? How?

_____
_____
_____
_____
_____
_____
_____
_____
_____

RAP = Read And Pray

Condemnation, Reconciliation, Redemption, Justification

Synopsis = Outline, Summary.
Condemnation means: Conviction, Judgment
Reconciliation means: Reunion, Resolution, Understanding.
Redemption means: Restored, Liberated, Exchange, Reclaimed.
Justification means: Defense, Reasoning, Confirmation.

Synopsis: Let's **sum up** where we have been, where we are and what happens in this thing we call 'life on earth".

Condemnation: We came naked and **condemned** to live in a world full of sin. The only place outside heaven where there is no sin is – nowhere. On the brighter side at the same time the new being is sealed in God's love until the age of accountability (determined by the level of knowledgeable reasoning.) After that time the _judgment_ is harsh with a heavy debt upon certain _conviction_.

Reconciliation: Because of this condemnation there comes a need for **reconciliation** to the time of innocence. There is an _understanding_ that a perfect _resolution_ is the only solution for a _reunion_ of the created to the Creator.

Redemption: With this **redemption** the guilty is pronounced _liberated_ and _reclaimed_ as a free person who has been _restored_ in exchange for the mercy and grace of the One who posted bail on the Cross of Calvary.

Justification: is the reward _confirming_ the _defense_ settled the score of all accusations of the prosecutor.

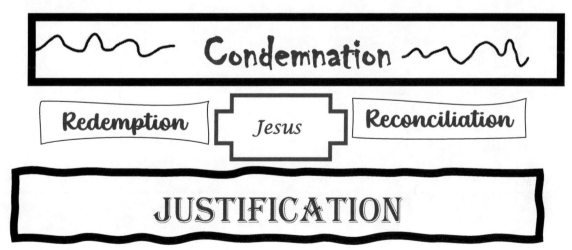

RAP = Read And Pray

What is the difference in:
Justification, Sanctification and Glorification?

(A) Justification is what happens the moment you accept Jesus Christ as your Savior and LORD of your life. The moment you are Born-Again. (a) All your sins are gone and forgiven. (b) You are sealed forever as a Child of God.

(B) Sanctification is what happens between that moment and the moment you die and see Jesus face-to-face. (a) Your old life is gone. (b) Your penalty for those sins has been paid in full. (c) However, you still have to live in a world full of sin. (d) You will never be alone or incapable of handling temptation because the Holy Spirit that is in you will be your counselor and guide. © You always keep learning and growing spiritually until the day you die. (f) You never graduate from the college of sanctifying until you are Glorified.

(C) Glorification is what happens for the rest of eternity in Heaven, living in a world without sin. (a) Glorification is the promise latched on to Sanctification. (b) You are welcomed into Heaven and can live forever in a world that knows no sin. (c) You are secure and full of joy, peace, and happiness; but, above those benefits – You are living with Jesus Christ in the presence of God *(with no fear)*.

Write out below, in your own words, the meaning of each:

Justification is:
_____
_____
_____

Sanctification is:
_____
_____
_____
_____
_____

Glorification is:
_____

RAP = Read And Pray

Justification

Justification happens in an instance and is totally an act of God. No one can justify their sins by calling the sin a legal act, or a happenstance, or blaming the devil for the act of sin committed. While it is true that the devil does tempt that causes sinful thought – always remember that he has no power to know what you will do with that thought until you act upon it. He reads actions – not thoughts. The only ALL knowing being is God Almighty.

A person is totally responsible for acting upon a thought. Neither God nor satan will force a person into something that is either right or wrong. Therefore, before a person can be justified in the sight of God, a personal choice has to be made. God holds no one prisoner from exercising their free will and satan does not have the power to do so. God offers liberty and freedom while satan offers torment. Shouldn't the choice of the first be the choice one would make? Who wishes upon themselves addiction to sin that brings torment?

One more point to drive that thought home and we will be done with giving satan the time of day. God *always* makes a way for a person to overcome satan's temptations but the person has to *look outside themselves* for deliverance. No one can be justified nor sanctified outside looking to Jesus Christ to be the deliverer. I repeat – 'No One'. Not the church tithe giver, not the do-gooder, not the kings, not the queens, not even you or me. It cannot be done. (How to solve this problem with faulty-thinking is dealt with, in much detail, in the section of this book under the Plan of Salvation.)

JUSTIFICATION by regeneration is a moment in the space of a life-time. <u>The moment</u> in that Sanctification begins. A person is transformed with power to live in an unholy world without taking part in that unholiness. And wait for it - "The act of Justification lasts for the rest of life on earth" whether that life span be a hundred years or just one day. Once salvation is given and received <u>it is sealed</u>. God validated it when Jesus paid the price. Is that too good to be true, you might ask? Say for instance that should it not be true – then, Christ would have to go back to the Cross of Calvary every single time a person sinned. From a Chrisitan's point of view, WHO would do such a thing to our Savior? Certainly, no one who has been redeemed and reconciled with God. Take this point in check – *"Neither would God allow it."*

There is great happiness and freedom for the person who knows that they are forgiven when they might mess up and cause another or themselves harm or shame. The word here to remember is willfully going against God's laws and being disobedient to the Father of truth. We are saved sinner. Since the point of your salvation have you done, said, applauded or laughed at sin, or taught anything that goes against being wholly holy? Uh oh. Did you as a result, run back to the Cross throw yourself in the blood and beg for forgiveness as if you are lost and never been forgiven? Could you live freely and at liberty if you nailed yourself to that Cross and refused to go forward and live a sanctified life from your point of salvation? Jesus does not need to be still hanging on the cross to fulfill your hope for salvation. Salvation didn't begin and end at the Cross because salvation was completed at the resurrection. He rose to a new life and that is what He wants for you.

One time on the Cross was enough for Jesus and one time on the Cross is enough for you. Who would dare insist that Jesus keep being crucified over and over every time one of God's children sin? Hear me, this wonderful security does not mean we must not ask for forgiveness from the point of salvation; certainly, we must confess and ask for forgiveness otherwise we would be out of fellowship with God Almighty.

For a person to continually beg for forgiveness and stomp in Jesus's blood usually means they have not repented, turned from their wicked way nor accepted Jesus as their savior to begin with. He didn't go to the Cross to stay there; He fulfilled it's purpose then rose to give us that same victory. At the beginning of the Church age, Jesus told His converted disciples to "go-ye" and that is what He wants us to do also. From that day forward we are to live humbly by owning up to our mistakes, confess them, turn from them, learn from them, and go forward in victory.

A person who feels like they can't keep themselves saved has never tasted salvation because it is still all about the person, not about the Savior. If there is a shred of doubt concerning reconciliation with God, then there is room to be sure. (go back to the plan of salvation). Otherwise, rejoice because all your sins have been forgiven. Receiving Jesus's blood sacrifice once is enough. Don't keep walking in it; but go through it to the Father.

The second-best day of a person's life is when they realize they cannot keep themselves saved. The best day of a person's life is when they allow themselves to be saved by the blood of Jesus to obtain peace with God. Trying to live holy without holiness is impossible. Self-righteousness is crippling but Jesus'-righteousness is freedom. There is no way to have the help of the Holy Spirit without going through Jesus to God. He, the Holy Spirit, makes living holy in an unholy world possible.

Early on we have talked about salvation and reconciliation with God and the next thing up is to understand justification. Justification is the point of contact to the living water, the door, and the good shepherd. For spiritual growth, it is important to exercise faith because without it no one can please God. As soon as your name is written in the Book of Life you are imbedded with a measure of faith. It's up to you to learn how to use this newfound faith and it's up to the Holy Spirit to guide you in exercising faith. Faith makes a person strong when they are weak. Advancing the Kingdom of God is your new job as a redeemed and justified Christian.

The first phase (Justification) *is the point of entry* into eternal life. Justification is accomplished in those who believe (repent and confess) that Jesus Christ is the Son of God, who came into this world to be our sacrifice for sin so that those who believe by faith are thereby given the right to go to heaven to be in God's favor and presence. This act of grace and mercy is wholly accomplished through acceptance of Jesus Christ who becomes our sacrifice for sins which we have committed against God.

*Justification is the instantaneous act of God whereby He forgives the sinner of all sins-past, present, and future-and declares him perfectly righteous in His sight.

*Justification is grounded on the gift of righteousness that God freely imputes to the believer at the moment of salvation. Read Romans 5:17; 2 Corinthians. 5:21; Philippians 3:9).

*Justification before a holy God is possible solely on the grounds that Christ has shouldered every sin committed by the sinner. Read Hebrews10:10-14; 1 Peter. 3:18).

*Justification is an act of pure love, grace and mercy which will freely attribute His perfect righteousness. Read Romans 3:21-26; 5:17; 2 Corinthians 5:21; Philippians 3:9; 1John 2:2).

*Justification is always by grace and never by works, as the sinner is justified through the redemption that is in Christ Jesus" (Romans 3:24).

> *"For all have sinned and come short*
> *of the glory of God;*
> *being justified freely by His grace*
> *through the redemption*
> *that is in Christ Jesus;"*
> Romans 3:23-24

Countless men and women of theological study have come to the same conclusion that some things are clearly indisputable when taught by none other than the Holy Spirit from the Holy Word of God. That is not to say that one denomination rules the roost. You know as well as I do that everyone has an opinion and is entitled to it. But keep one thing in mind as you study. Ask yourself: "do I believe this because it is true; or is it true (to me) because I believe it?" All people can believe a lie at some point but that never makes it true. Be guided by the Holy Spirit always in every decision. He charges nothing and is all available to the Christian. His advice is just one of the free benefits.

RAP = Read And Pray

A synopsis of the second phase (Sanctification) and the third phase (Glorification) will be useful at this point of study as to know what to expect from now to death and what will take place at death when one enters into Life everlasting.

The second phase (Sanctification) *is the journey* of salvation and this phase takes place from salvation to earthly death of the believer and this will be discussed in detail in the pages to come. Here is a sampling of the facts concerning sanctification that offer Scriptural back-references:

*Sanctification is the process whereby the believer moves from spiritual infancy to spiritual maturity over time as he/she learns God's Word and makes good choices to live God's will Read Ephesians 4:11-16; 2 Thessalonians 2:13; 2 Timothy 3:14-17; 1 Peter 2:2; 2 Peter 3:18.

*Sanctification allows the Christian to advance in spiritual maturity and does so only by the power of the Holy Spirit and on the basis of God's Word which is to be daily learned and applied. Read Ephesians 5:18; Galatians. 5:16; 1 Peter 2:2; 2 Peter 3:18.

The third Phase (Glorification) *is the destination*. Heaven is not about receiving a mansion in the sky; it is however about living with Jesus forever in God's House, as a redeemed Child of The King.

"Glorification is the final phase of the believer's experience and occurs when he/she leaves this world, either by death or by rapture, and enters into the presence of God in heaven Read Romans 8:17-18.

*Glorification is when the Christian achieves sinless perfection. This happens upon entry into heaven at which time a new body is given which will last for eternity. Read Philippians. 3:20-21.

*Justification (Regeneration by re-birth) *is the point of entry into eternal* **life**.
*Sanctification is *the journey* while on earth.
*Glorification is *the destination* achieved and finalized upon arrival in heaven.

Notes:_____
_____
_____
_____
_____
_____

RAP = Read And Pray

Sanctification

The act of sanctification is a fascinating amazing journey. By this time an individual has suffered through condemnation, has been redeemed by reconciliation and received the instant reward of forgiveness. That in itself is quite an accomplishment seeing that it was all an act of God, without that would be an impossible endeavor.

For the purpose of this study, we will spend more time on the word "Sanctification", then on the words "Justification" and "Glorification" because the first period of a person's life is spent trying to find justification to satisfy the debt due for sins we committed. Though this period of time is not readily visible for those who wander around trying to find satisfaction in living in all kinds of ways that do not satisfy the soul. From the point of being held accountable for oneself to the point of justification, a lot of time can be wasted in vanity and vexation of living. There is no true joy in the soul. Those given over to this unjustified jail sentence are of all men and women most miserable. These have not yet tasted victory over satan.

This type of study is not meant to alienate the unsaved person but rather meant to include such because investigation into the Word of God brings unexpected liberation from the prison where they hold their own key to freedom. This surrender is not for losers because this type of surrender is victory and brings freedom. No bail, no fees, no sacrifice other than acceptance of God's plan to salvation.

The unsaved cannot be a part of Sanctification. They have to pass through Justification first. Therefore, this study into the act of Sanctifying (to make holy, purifying, dedicating, blessing) is only meant for those who have been Justified through the sacrifice of Jesus Christ. Otherwise, they are lost as a ball in high weeds in understanding the things possible and permanently granted to the saints who became saints out of the pure mercy and grace of God. A saint never boasts that he/she has been granted sainthood. Nobody earned sainthood – it is a gift of God..

Let me add at this point that a gift is not a gift if it can be taken away again. A true gift holds no strings by the giver. This is why once received, and a person has signed for the gift – it can never be taken away. It now belongs to the recipient. There is plenty of truth to this fact in the Bible and I could chase this rabbit for a long time. However, let's let this unfold as we begin to understand the act of *Sanctification*.

RAP = Read And Pray

Qualification of Sanctification

The very first step toward sanctifying is realizing it has nothing to do with you – but rather all to do with the capabilities of Jesus Christ' redeeming blood sacrifice and the keeping power of the Holy Spirit. That fact alone should take the pressure off a person who might be tempted to think they cannot live the life expected of someone who calls himself or herself a Christian. The doubts of the looming "what ifs" have to go bye-bye. Go ahead, salute it, then send your doubts packing because you are no longer just a person struggling through life the best you can with self-justification looming over your head. Self-justification is always transparent. It fools no one. To become a Christian one is granted the power to become Christ-like. The Holy Spirit will spend the rest of your life with you. And He is the only One who can give you power to overcome the temptations you will face as a Christian. Without Him, the act of sanctifying would be impossible because even though we are saved we have to continue to live in a world full of sin.

Sanctification happens on earth, in a place full of sin.
This process takes place on earth.
We graduate to being Glorified when we die on earth
and take the next step to a world without sin, called Heaven.

Heaven is your destination because you are a Child of The King of Kings and the Lord of Lords. You have been given this rank because of accepting Jesus Christ as your sacrifice and His blood has paid the debt you owed and could not pay.

This King always has your back. He has destroyed the condemnations of the past by assuring you of sainthood, even while living in an unholy world. That is not something to hide in the closet. Sanctification actually comes from the word *Saint*, which involves sainthood and means "a very virtuous, kind, or patient person who is acknowledged as "holy." You are probably thinking but He is still working on us, and that is so true. We cannot live holy all the time and neither should we boast or give the impression of being a "holier than thou" kind of person.

After a person has been justified to see God face to face – then and only then do you start the course of sanctification. And that process will be ongoing for the rest of life on earth. The only short cut to this process is if God saved you one moment and then you died the next or immediately be caught up in the rapture of the Church. In events such as these the process of sanctification is skipped because you would automatically be Glorified and in God's presence. That is what Justification does – it sends you to heaven. Those benefits are ready to receive for the asking.

The best thing I've ever done is to die to myself and live in Christ Jesus. That knowledge of who I am is what sustains me in tough times. Situations cannot scrub the love of God off me. I'm sealed at every corner. While tempted, I still have power to resist and overcome.

RAP = Read And Pray

Not of myself; I repeat. But rather power to resist because of the gift of the Holy Spirit who is responsible for my sanctification. It is a total new rebuild and not a remodeling of an old self. It is being a new being all because of the born-again experience. That is where eternal life starts. Otherwise, outside of salvation a person lives in an eternal-death state of being.

So, in light of these facts, it is established that sanctification is a lifelong process, not a destination of itself. It begins with salvation and ends at Glorification. By being glorified, we obtain Sainthood. We graduate. We get a diploma. We are an alumnus of the process of sanctification. Not good works, not generosity, not even kindness can *save* a person. It is an act of God. Period. He knows who graduates to eternal life.

Yes, there is something that everyone must do and that something is simply to surrender oneself and allow God to inhabit their being through belief in His Son, Jesus Christ. This is evident by confessing sin and turning away from it. This is the beginning work of Sanctification. Sanctification to me is: "living daily in the power of God's love and grace, under the guidance of the Holy Spirit."

What does sanctification mean to you?

Are you in the midst of being sanctified?

Does that process sometimes hurt?

RAP = Read And Pray

The Duty of Sanctification

When my husband served in the military stationed at Homestead Air Force Base, I worked for a fruit packing plant in Florida. Part of my duty as an employee was sorting lemons on a conveyer belt. The objective was to get the rotten ones away from the good ones. Simply put. I admit it took a little time to recognize that ones to toss into the rejection bucket. In a short time I recognized those lemons of sub-quality the moment they touched the belt. However, sometimes in my haste I rejected a good one and let a bad one slip in to go to market.

Sanctification is such, really. Your duty is to recognize the good things and reject the infectious lies that satan plants as hinderances. Up front, recognize that satan is the god of this world and will try to slip in and split up the progression of sanctification by hindering the work of the Holy Spirit. Our bodies, emotions, minds, and many relationships have been spoiled by touching and tasting contaminated fruit which should have been thrown in the trash can. It starts with thoughts and if those thoughts are not rejected and thrown into the rejection bucket they will fester and spoil the best of relationships. The most important relationship which will be hindered is fellowship with God.

The duty that rests upon the Holy Spirit, involving the process of sanctification, can be a slow process but during this time many good things can happen such as a reliance upon God's power rather than our own. When a relationship is healthy it has room to flourish and becomes even more beautiful than at the onset. People do not enjoy living in a place outside their element. When the Holy Spirit moves into the life of a new Christian, everything about that person's thinking, habits and desire is exposed to Him, for better or worst. From that day forward the Christian must see himself through the eyes of God – in the way God sees him or her and allows God to change habits to become in Jesus's likeness.

You see, many young Christians have never experienced this kind of relationship with anyone. It can be confusing, maybe even intimidating when we see ourselves through God's eyes. Just you think! The Creator loves you – fully and unconditionally. He would never save a person from a burning hell and then say to that person, "you go now and make it the best you can for the rest of your life on earth, I'm busy." On the contrary, He says just the opposite. He says; "I'm assigning the Holy Spirit to start His duty of sanctifying you to be fit for the Kingdom." Yes indeed, sanctification is a beautiful on-going thing. To understand this is vital for a thriving Christian's life. It also has many twists and turns, and one size does not fit all. It's deeply personal and tailored to the individual.

I raised a son and shared in the lives of five grandsons. During periods of their young lives they especially loved the transformers toys that looks and functions changed drastically with a few twists and turns. You could take an action figure and transform that same toy into a vehicle of some kind with a totally different purpose. As a Christian, God has already taken the sinner person that you are and transformed you into something that sees things you perhaps have never seen before. You still have all the same features you have always had but your purpose is entirely different and you don't even know what you are capable of doing in the hands of the Master. I saw my grandsons' eyes widen in disbelief when toys changed into something they were not. They delighted in moving the parts back and forth, back, and forth. Sanctification is not a child's play toy. Do you see? It is different with Christianity because in this newfound identity, Christians don't want to return to what they were. This change of being works best in the hands of the Master. He should have total control because He is responsible for you now and is faithful to do any and all fine-tuning to make you the best possible servant for His Kingdom.

> *"Sanctify them through thy truth; thy word is truth.*
> *As thou hast sent me into the world, even so have I sent them*
> *into the world. And for their sakes I sanctify myself,*
> *that they also might be sanctified through the truth.*
> *Neither pray I for these alone,*
> *but for them also that shall believe on me through their word."*
> *John 17:17-19*

Take some time to focus of the above Scripture and realize – Jesus prayed for you, - yes you! He knows that sin leaves scars. His hands, feet, back, and head bore them beautifully and gracefully. He was not a sinner, but rather He was the antidote for sin. He is still the cure, solution, remedy, and answer to stop the madness and give the relief. So, don't live like you do not have the power to be an overcomer; because you do. You do because you obtained grace.

G R A C E
<u>G</u>od's
<u>R</u>iches
<u>A</u>t
<u>C</u>hrist'
<u>E</u>xpense.

No one has to be a Christian for twenty years or more in order to be considered a saint. Sainthood is a gift just as surely as is salvation and even the newest believer is considered a "saint". Not by merit, but by gift. Therefore it is the saint's responsibility to grow in the process of sanctification for the duration of life on earth. Somewhere we got the notion that to be a saint one had to see themselves as 'saintly'. Again, it is not about how we see ourselves – it is about how God sees us. It's His doings, not ours. We are just sinners who have been saved by grace and kept by the mercy of Jesus Christ. Let God call us what He will. Do not fret over things that are God's business; for He is always in control and involved in His children's day to day lives. He is not an absentee Father. He is your loving Father.

RAP = Read And Pray

The Habitation of Sanctification

After picking my children up from an after-school event it was dark when I approached our mailbox by the roadside but just before I was to make the turn into the driveway I noticed something out of the ordinary. I could see a vehicle in the shadows and a figure of a man going into the house. My husband was not due home from work for another couple hours. We lived in the country and did not have any close neighbors however there was a church nearby so I drove pass my turn to the parking lot of the church where I could take a closer look without being spotted by the intruder. My heart was racing, as I watched to see what the man might do. My imagination began to run wild as I visualized him ransacking every room. Soon he turned on the light and stepped out onto the porch so I could identify that it was not an intruder, but indeed it was my husband who was home early. The fear I felt when I thought someone was trying to get into my home uninvited, quickly turned to relief. I was so happy it was my husband who was in the house.

As a Christian, someone is in your house. He was invited in and has been given a key to the door of your heart. He belongs there and his ever-abiding presence should be a great comfort to you. Yet sometimes we treat Him in an unwelcome fashion. There may even be places of the heart and mind where He is not welcomed. We cannot trust Jesus to save us from the flames of hell and not trust the Holy Spirit enough to look in all our closets. In the process of sanctification The Holy Spirit must be an Inhabitant and have access to every nook and cranny. No one can live a fully satisfying life in Christ if the Holy Spirit is not welcome to sweep the crumbs from under the rugs as well as control the thermostat and make Himself at home.

The new believer may just be getting used to being justified by faith when they suddenly are nervously aware of just what that means. It means you have surrendered the master key to The Master and He knows your business and all your going and coming. He has the right of permanent inhabitation. There is a new occupant in the house. That is a tremendously wonderful thing, but let's admit it can also be a little intimidating because one knows they cannot be super good – *all the time*. What about if we want to watch the ball games all day on Saturday instead of preparing to teach a class on Sunday morning? I'm messing with you a little; but how true is that?

This new inhabitant is not demanding nor judgmental. Jesus said He did not come to judge the world but that the world through Him might be saved. He is in the house as our security system. The sooner we learn that we are secure in His love, the sooner we will grow and mature in that love and willingly be obedient when He gives us instructions on what to do in order to advance His Kingdom. Jesus should never be the just the the doormat to wipe our shoes on when He owns the home. And He shouldn't be the mop to clean up our messes; yet He does. Your spiritual house can be cold and unwelcoming or warm with thanksgiving and gratitude. It is up to us what kind of dwelling we welcome Jesus into.

RAP = Read And Pray

Sanctification in part is recognizing that our redemption has been accomplished by Christ alone, and part realizing that our redemption is functional by the Spirit that dwells within us. Jesus promised His disciples that the Father would send the Holy Spirit to dwell among and in the believers as a guiding counselor. Jesus could not permanently dwell on the earth in person form; but the Holy Spirit can dwell within the believer as a permanent resident.

As Christians start to understand the profound nature of the union with Jesus, then they must also begin to see the enormous riches available for spiritual growth in Christlikeness.

The Holy Spirit's work of sanctification requires Him to be in-house at all times. We cannot do this act of being sanctified unattended. His presence brings enjoyment, delight and adoration for God the Father and Jesus the Son. The trinity does the work that only comes about with habitation of all three person in the sanctification process. As we believe the reality of the Trinity Godhead, we also must recognize that we are 100% responsible, yet 100% dependent on the help of the inhabitants that came to reside by invitation at the point of salvation.

"For I know whom I have believed and am persuaded that he is able to keep that which I have committed unto him against that day. Hold fast the form of sound words, which thou hast heard of me, in faith and love which is in Christ Jesus. That good thing which was committed unto thee keep by the Holy Ghost which dwelleth in us." 2 Timothy 1:12-14

"And grieve not the holy Spirit of God, whereby ye are sealed unto the day of redemption." Ephesians 4:30

"What? Know ye not that your body is the temple of the Holy Ghost, which is in you, which ye have of God, and ye are not your own?" 1 Corinthians 6:19

"(But this spake he of the Spirit, which they that believe on him should receive for the Holy Ghost was not yet given; because that Jesus was not yet glorified.) John :39

"But the Comforter, which is the Holy Ghost, whom the Father will send in my name, he shall teach you all things, and bring all things to your remembrance, whatsoever I have said unto you. Peace I leave with you, my peace I give unto you: not as the world giveth, give I unto you. Let not your heart be troubled, neither let it be afraid." John 14:26-27

"Go ye therefore, and teach all nations, baptizing them in the name of the Father, and of the Son, and of the Holy Ghost: teaching them to observe all things whatsoever I have commanded you: and, lo, I am with you always, even unto the end of the world." Amen. Matthew 28:19-20

RAP = Read And Pray

*"If Christ is in you,
although the body is dead because of sin,
the Spirit is life because of righteousness."*
Galatians 2:20

*"I have been crucified with Christ.
It is no longer I who live, but Christ who lives in me."*
Romans 8:10

Use the space below to express your views of the habitation of the Holy Spirit doing the work of Sanctification:

Notes:

RAP = Read And Pray

The Security of Sanctification

It is the duty and responsibility of the believer to be actively and personally involved with the process of sanctification and to recognize that we are sanctified only by the habitation of The Trinity. This should not be a stressful endeavor, to the contrary It should be a relief.

I was an employee of the public school system for twenty-eight years and during that time part of my duty allowed me to be in any school at any time involving inventory and fixed assets. My nephew attended one of these schools and word got back to me that he was involved in some minor mischief. Knowing that was not his character I went to his classroom and called him out into the hall where I commenced to give him an aunt's point of finger and going so far as to let him know that I would always find out what he was doing. After that day all I needed to do was 'give him that look' and he would start confessing to things he thought I was already aware.

In our relationship with God, we might as well go ahead and confess our sin in its moment so that the Holy Spirit can help us come clean of it. Then it is our responsibility to chalk it up as sin, know we are forgiven and commit to never do it again. Otherwise a condition known as back-sliding takes over. The misery will be a life out of fellowship with God and wasted because the act of sanctification is hindered. We, not God, pulled the plug of spiritual growth. From that point we miss the best of the best of life on earth. That is not God's plan.

After my husband passed away I was lost without him, and I understood my life was over as I had known it for forty-six years. My day-to-day world was shattered. During this period of grief I came to one conclusion. That was to find God's *divine* will for my life. I told Him I would not be satisfied with His permissive will; but I wanted to be smack in the middle of His divine will and I did not know what that was, but He did. In time, during the process, I got many confirmations from Him that He was at work making that happen. I was determined to not butt-in with His business of setting things in order, while He was opening doors and helping me understand that *His Way* was to be my way as well. I have been truly amazed at what He has done in my life since that time.

One thing to remember while in a state of being sanctified (until death you do depart) is to always gage actions to be in line with God's standards. It is up to you to develop a regular time of Bible Study and Prayer and to make this a priority. Security in sanctification is the greatest of all blessings for every human being. Remember, let's repeat: We are saved by G R A C E - that is God's Riches At Christ' Expense.

RAP = Read And Pray

While my destination changed amidst what I thought would be forever; Jesus' mission and destination never changed. The Cross was where He was headed, and He knew it. Neither did He need *to surrender* to the road ahead of Him, because God's divine plan was always Jesus' plan from the very beginning. Knowledge that He was headed to the Cross of Calvary did not prevent Him from enjoying His earthly family and friends during the time He wore sandals on His feet. He never lived a day in dread of tomorrow and I say this because I'm sure having come from Heaven He was indeed ready to go back to be with His Father. Living with his family of earth was a time to assure us that He understands what it means to have family and also the challenges that come with it.

God's *divine will* did not cease when Jesus had nails in His hands and feet. On the contrary, God's (divine) will was being done at that very moment. Jesus was meek as a lamb and strong as a lion at the same time. Meekness actually means, Strength under control. For three years he had been on the mission of ministry like none other ever before or after. He was showing the world who His Father (God) was and lived His *divine will* daily.

My words are meeting the keyboard forming this page on a Palm Sunday. It's almost as if I can smell the streets of that day when Jesus entered into Jerusalem riding a donkey.

Just one week in the span of time – Changed Everything.

Let's assume it was Sunday, April 2, in the year 30 A.D. (Some scholars think Jesus was born 3 to 5 years before A.D. began.) Nevertheless, for here we will call that day – The Day of His Triumphant Entry into Jerusalem. He and His followers made quite a stir when he entered into Jerusalem riding on a donkey with people shouting praises and putting palm leaves and clothing on the path such as a red carpet might be rolled out for a very important diplomat or famous person. (See Luke 19 and John 12) Jesus knew where this path was going to lead, and He did not shy away from it. He didn't try to hide in the crowd or disguise Himself. He accepted the praise. Soon this praise would turn to protest. It would only be after the resurrection that the people would understand the magnitude of the triumphal entry. All prophecy was fulfilled in Jesus Christ as *The Messiah*. However, even the ones who knew the messianic prophecies the best - rejected Jesus claiming Him to be a fraud.

Monday, April 3rd. = Two significant events happened. *The Cursing of the Fig Tree and the Cleansing of the Temple. (See* Mark 11, Hosea 9:10, Jeremiah 7:11) Indicating that the Christian should not be found lacking in producing fruit for God's glory. And The temple was a place set aside for God's glory and not turned into a bazaar for personal financial gain.

Tuesday, April 4th. A day of Controversy and Teaching. That morning Jesus and his disciples discovered the fig tree withered. The religious leaders tried to trap and embarrass Him, but Jesus used His wisdom and knowledge of the Scriptures for His defense. The Scribes and Pharisees were condemned. Jesus sat on the Mount of Olives and predicted the destruction of the temple. (See Mark 13).

RAP = Read And Pray

Wednesday, April 5th. Judas' Betrayal. The Gospel did not record Jesus' activities for that day that is why it is sometimes called "silent Wednesday". Judas probably used this opportunity to venture into Jerusalem to plan the denial. The religious leaders had been looking for a way and a time to capture Jesus. Judas found a way for this to be done away from the crowd of Jesus' supporters.

Thursday, April 6th. The Last Supper. That evening Jesus would gather with His disciples in an upper room of a home in Jerusalem. (See John 13). Jesus predicted that Peter would deny Him and one of the disciples would betray Him. At some point in the middle of that night, Jesus, and His disciples (minus Judas) walked to the garden of Gethsemane for a time of prayer. (See Mark 14:32-50) The time was interrupted as Judas led a group of Jesus's opponents to arrest Him. Here the disciples abandoned Jesus.

Friday, April 7th. The Crucifixion of The Son of God. Throughout the rest of the night and early morning Jesus was put to trial and accused of blasphemy. He was beaten mercilessly, ridiculed, spat upon, mocked, and taunted, then crucified. (See John 18 and 19, Mark 14 and 15, Luke 23) To know the extent of this torture is to learn Roman culture and practices of that day. Utterly horrendous acts upon our Savior, Jesus Christ. The guiltless Son of God. From 12 p.m. until 3 p.m., darkness covered all the land. At three o'clock, Jesus died and committed His spirit into the hands of His Father, saying "It is finished." His dead body was taken down and placed in a borrowed tomb.

Saturday, April 8th. The disciples hid away, and fear gripped the Pharisees because of the words of Jesus that in three days He would rise again. (See Matt. 27:63)

Sunday, April 9th. The Resurrection of Jesus Christ. The tomb was found empty, the stone was rolled away, and the angel of the Lord spoke. (See Luke 24). Jesus appeared to Mary Magdelene and to two disciples on the road to Emmaus and later in the day to His disciples who were in hiding. (See John 20, Luke 24)

The sun set that glorious day and the world had changed. Life everlasting was available to all – free of charge – because the sin debt had been paid by the perfect spotless lamb. The Lamb was our Sacrifice. But the Victory came three days later. Our salvation hinges on the truth of Resurrection!. That my friend, is how you and I can live confidently in the Security of Sanctification.

Victory came three days later.
Salvation hinges on the resurrection!
As He rose to new life, As Christians so shall we!

Jesus didn't try to change His course to suit anyone, nor should you. Don't think for a second that being secure in Jesus means you can let down your guard and live recklessly tethering on the edge or tempting Jesus to accept legalized sin, just because the world says it is ok.. That is preposterous. Jesus is not tempted to sin, and He will not tempt anyone to sin. If sin is a temptation, rest assured that temptation did not come from Jesus Christ. So, where then? It came from the father of lies, satan himself.

Because of that inescapable fact, who does satan like to mess with? Is it those who have not been justified? Those who have not walked the salvation bridge to freedom? No, because they are perfectly capable of sinning all by themselves and we should not give satan more recognition that he deserves. He messes with those being sanctified more than the unjustified because his greatest pleasure is to bring shame to The Son of God. What could be more shameful to God Almighty than to see those who claimed salvation – turn again to sin - by not using the God given Holy Spirit, The Word of God and Prayer to be overcomers of the world and its temptations? Satan is conniving and always scheming up ways to place doubts and fears in the believers' thoughts. When this happens to you, recognize it is satan and call on the Holy Spirit for help and deliverance. Satan puts thoughts in the mind because of lust for us to be something we are not. The thing we often fail to recognize is that satan cannot read our mind because he is not all-knowing. Only God is all knowing. He knows he has won this round only when he sees our actions.

For anyone to think they can live the rest of their life on earth (after salvation) without the process of being sanctified is ridiculous. If that were so, then we would just skip sanctification altogether and go straight to being *Glorified*. (To be Glorified is living holy in a holy world; while to be Sanctified is to live holy in an unholy world). Without the process of daily sanctification we all would be saved (justified) and immediately die and go to heaven. That way we would have no need to learn about Sanctification and how to be overcomers in a world full of sin. Sanctification is in the middle of being justified and being glorified. Sanctification is who we are in Christ Jesus and is how we live day to day with Godly wisdom and Godly power to be overcomers.

The Christian must quit seeing Jesus the way they want to and instead start seeing Him for <u>Who He is</u>. He is not waiting in the corner for us to learn the hard lessons all on our own. He is not waiting in the closet as your crutch waiting for you to break a leg and use Him only after you've fallen and can't get up by yourself. He is not the pot of gold at the end of a rainbow as you take chances of gambling with life. And He is not proud of those who wabble through life on their own thinking they are saved and not going to hell so that's enough. On the contrary He is enough. He is enough to help you live life without fear of tomorrow. He is enough to give you joy in the midst of tragedy. He is enough to shower you with miracles and prosperity. And He certainly is enough to be your deliverance or antidote to satan' conniving vices. This is all His work as He does for us what we cannot do without Him.

Isn't sanctification the most beautiful thing you have ever seen? If you have been redeemed go to the nearest mirror, look at yourself and ask: "is this the face of someone who is living as one who has been redeemed by Jesus Christ? Is there anything I'm involved in that takes the glow of salvation from my countenance?" If that mirror doesn't reflect inner joy then you are hindering God's work of sanctifying you. Why am I saying this? Because at times I've looked in the mirror at myself. There are times I have disappointed God and it shows not only to me in the mirror but to the world around me as well.

When a tough situation comes around, take a moment, and think: *"How I handle this will either help or hinder my spiritual growth."* The wise Christian is ever growing and maturing in understanding and Godly wisdom.

> *"But the wisdom that is from above is first pure, then peaceable, gentle, and easy to be instead, full of mercy and good fruits, without partiality, and without hypocrisy."* James 3:17

Let us remember that not only did Jesus die in order for our sins to be forgiven through his sacrifice, but He also took our shame and humiliation while on the Cross. There is not any circumstance of torture and agony that Jesus cannot relate to. Consider the following words of Michael Kelley who wrote:

"While Jesus hung on the cross, a soldier offered Him something to drink. Despite what we might imagine, this act was not intended to comfort Jesus but to demonstrate contempt. Jesus was parched: soldiers held to His lips a sponge on the end of a stick (See Matthew 27:48; John 9:28-29). The moment they did this, the crowds likely roared with laughter. Public stone-constructed latrines were common in the first-century world. Those using the facilities sat on stone benches that had strategically placed holes in them. Below the peoples' feet flowed water through a trough. People used a sponge on the end of a stick as their "toilet paper" and afterward rinsed the sponge in the flowing water. Whether or not this sponge had ever been used for this purpose would not have mattered. The imagery was the same. Rather than relief Jesus was ridiculed - rather than helped, humiliation."

Those who think that Jesus does not know how torture and humiliation feels, does not know the nature of God's love. Could God really love Jesus and allow Him such humiliation? God's love was not only focused on His Son, but it was also focused on all of humanity. That includes me and you. He loves us that much also.

Consider: Because of the love God has for you and me; He was willing to allow His Son to take our shame, be our pain, and bear our burdens because if each of us had to die the same kind of death Jesus did; then we would "just be dead", However, because Jesus was the One and Only perfect sacrifice it was God's plan for Jesus to take our punishment for sin. No person has the right to think or say that God is not perfect love. Quickly before we lose this thought, let's add another: It was God's plan, Jesus always knew this plan and did not try to think up a way to get out of it.

RAP = Read And Pray

Jesus' divine will was to do God's divine will. They were in this together from the beginning and Jesus did not die because an angry mob tortured Him. He died for my sins and yours, willingly. He took our punishment and bore our pain. Oh, that the world could understand the truth in this! But the world (that has not been redeemed) believes Jesus to be whom they want Him to be – not who He really is.

Record your thoughts and notes below:

RAP = Read And Pray

The Demonstration of Sanctification

As the process of being sanctified becomes a way of life in daily living certain things happen. One of these things is a ready recognition that you are not alone in this world, no matter how lonely you may feel during periods of sadness. Sadness for a Christian is a short narrow room with an open door at the end. How long we snooze in the room is up to us. I've been in this room many times. After my mother passed away when I was twenty years old, I stayed there for the longest time. My heart was shattered to a million pieces and for a while I didn't even see the open door. Praying was practically impossible. What I didn't realize during this storm of my life there was people outside my pass-through room who had me covered under their prayer umbrella. Not only that – the Holy Spirit was praying my prayer without me saying a word.

"Confess your faults one to another,
and pray one for another, that ye may be healed."
James 5:16

"Likewise the (Holy) Spirit also helpeth our infirmities:
for we know not what we should pray for as we ought:
but the (Holy) Spirit itself maketh intercession for us
with groanings that cannot be uttered."
Romans 8:26

Since that time, my father, four brothers, two sisters, my husband, a granddaughter and other family members and dear friends have died. Every single time I passed through this room (called grief) and had to rely on strength outside myself to get by. Every soul placed inside a baby is in eternity already. What we do in this clay shell determines where the eternal leads. One of two places, as you know. This is why the process of sanctification is so important. It teaches us the joy in Christ Jesus is far better than retaining earthly happiness.

The demonstrated sanctification of the saved-by-grace is a lifelong experience of joy and God-given mercy laced with faith and trust that comes with plenty of joy and miracles. It is a journey of twist and turns, ups and downs, and plenty of excitement watching God do what only God can do in your life. He demonstrates daily His Power, His ever-present Being and His all-knowing wisdom.

Below name one thing you have seen God do what only God can do in your own life?

RAP = Read And Pray

The End of Sanctification

One is never too old to quit learning how to live holy on this earth that we call home. Just as you might have told a small child to do or not to do something, they sometimes would do the very thing that you told them not to do. Perhaps, you even said a time or two – " I'm not telling you again!" But you did. You continued to tell them time and again the very same thing you said you would not say again.

Paul, yes even Paul, the writer of over half the New Testament who saw and talked with Jesus (after His ascension) – was as David in the Old Testament who was God's beloved and after His own heart. Both these totally (100% human) human beings had a little trouble sometimes and a lot of trouble other times during their own sanctification.

"For we know that the law is spiritual: but I am carnal, sold under sin. For that that I do I allow not: for what I would that do I not; but what I hate, that do I. If then I do that that I would not, I consent unto the law that it is good, Now then it is no more I that do it, but sin that dwelleth in me. For I know that in me (that is, in my flesh dwelleth no good thing: for to will is present with me; but how to perform that that is good I find not. For the good that I would I do not: but the evil that I would not that I do." Romans 7:14-19

In other words he was saying that even after the fact of salvation, he still struggled to do good. He wanted to always do good but found himself doing those things that he didn't want to do because sin was always an opportunity, and his flesh was sinful. He was still carnal (sensual) because he was not yet 'glorified'.

As far as King David was concerned, we can find evidence in the Book of Samuel just how sinful he was even though he loved God and God loved him – he was still living in a fleshly body. David did not confess his sin with Bathsheba until he was exposed by Nathan the Prophet. (Read 2 Samuel 12) Therefore, let us not think for a skinny second that we can live holy without the process of sanctification. God knew He would have to put us through this process during our life while we were still on earth because even the strongest fail to always live holy. He also, because of His love, mercy, and grace, gives us regular glimpses of what a world without sin will look like as a world where all is glorified in His presence and small visions of heaven.

I will even go so far as to say if, just if, there is a person living today who has not sinned after being saved, I cannot count myself as one of the perfectly perfect, and I know no one who has a right to claim such either. Write this down, in your memory-book: "no one has to be saved (justified/redeemed) more than once." Once is enough, if one is sure they were in the room when it happened. For Paul and David (and us) confession is the key to learning during the process of being sanctified. An unconfessed sin is torture on earth. There will be an unsettling in the soul that is not remedied until confessed and one turns away from the sin. Sin and guilt start bleeding of the soul. Because the soul is injured and will continue

RAP = Read And Pray

to hurt until the fellowship with God is restored. Don't be fooled, God will not allow total intimacy with Him if unconfessed sin continues to be in the camp. A person does not want to die in that condition and face God without a crown worthy to give Jesus. Of all people – these are the ones most miserable. Again, to continue in this life of sin is evidence that there is reason to question one's heart as to whether or not they have ever been saved. God will not be mocked.

"Be not deceived; God is not mocked: for whatsoever a man soweth, that shall he also reap. For he that soweth to his flesh shall of the flesh reap corruption; but he that soweth to the Spirit shall of the Spirit reap life everlasting. And let us not be weary in well doing for in due season we shall reap, if we faint not." Galatians 6:7-9

Because of so many difference denominations in Church membership Christians can receive, not received, or determine some theology as misinterpreted or unfounded based on personal opinion. It is not our jobs to straighten anyone out or slap any hands. Peter and the other Apostles found themselves in hot water, as the new church age was beginning. During one such time a doctor of the law, Gamaliel by name, had to stand up in defense by saying to an angry mob: -

"Ye men of Israel, take heed to yourselves what ye intend to do as touching these men. For before these days rose up Theudas, boasting himself to be somebody; to whom a number of men, about four hundred, joined themselves: who was slain; and all, as many an obeyed him, were scattered, and brought to naught. After this man rose up Judas of Galilee in the days of the taxing and drew away many people after him: He also perished; and all, even as many as obeyed him, were dispersed. And now I say unto you, Refrain from these men, and let them alone: for is this counsel of this work be of men, it will come to naught: but if it be of God, ye cannot overthrow it; lest haply ye be found even to fight against God." Acts 5:34-39

Paul also reminded the Philippians to – *"work out your own salvation with fear and trembling. For it is God that worketh in you both to will and to do of His good pleasure. Do all things without murmurings and disputing:"* Philippians 2:12-14

It should be our goal in growing in grace and understanding to seek out answers through personal Bible study and prayer. And let the Holy Spirit reveal the truth to your soul.

No matter how many good preachers you hear or how many revivals you attend – You must seek the truth for yourself. That means a little effort of sitting in God's presence while He opens your understanding. If all you know about God is what someone else has told you then ask yourself just how much trust you can put in a man or woman who is capable of falling (such as strong people like King David and Peter, etc.) and carrying others down with him or her?

RAP = Read And Pray

This is the very reason why so much time is given in this workbook to learn through regular personal Bible Study and Prayer (Read And Pray). And also why so much time is taken up explaining the worth of Sanctification. Sanctification meets us where we are and progresses according to commitment and sacrifice. As the old saying goes, "anything worth having is worth working for". Sanctification is the greatest thing to achieve. It means God is working on you and has worked hard to mold and make you into a fit vessel for heaven's sake. While salvation is a once and done thing – being sanctified puts us in the kilt which solidifies our relationship with God.

My brother and sister-in-law owned a ceramic shop. I put my hand to the clay and usually made a mess of it. I needed their help to re-do parts of my cup or saucer of whatever I was working on. It was a relief when they placed it into the heated kilt for finishing. It would be baked and when it came out of the heat it was not as fragile and it could now be used. I look at my soul in such a way. I still need some fine tuning. I trust God to be the one who is responsible for holding me securely because He will never drop me or lose me in this chaotic world. I can trust Him, and I can trust His judgment.

God sometimes has no choice but to put the wayward sinner who has been saved by grace back on the potter wheel. He will not throw your mess of life away – He will remold you.

> "O house of Israel, cannot I do with you as this potter?
> Saith the LORD. Behold, as the clay is in the potter's hand,
> so are ye in mine hand, O house of Israel.
> Jeremiah 18:6"

Let us not confuse our need to go back to the wheel with our need to go to the Cross. Going to the Cross has to come first. No one has a right to doubt your salvation, except you. God never saved anyone without letting them know. He never gave anyone the indwelling Holy Spirit without also giving knowledge to that person that someone new is in the house of the soul. There is confidence in salvation. If a person has no confidence in God's keeping power then perhaps there is no confidence in Jesus' saving power either.

How much has God had to say to me and you the very same thing over and over? Maybe God said to the angels in heaven – "that child of mine! When is he/she ever going to learn"? Well, that is what sanctification means, and it never ends as long as we breathe oxygen. It doesn't mean we are ever in danger of losing our salvation; but it does mean God never quits working on us while sanctifying us. When the process of sanctifying ends, it means you are headed to your eternal home, either heaven or hell. Preferably, of course, we go to peace and joy of heaven; rather than the eternal torment of hell. Do not waste valuable time trying to convince others of their errors. That is not your job. Your job is to willingly let the Master mold you and put you in the kilt when necessary.

RAP = Read And Pray

"Flee also youthful lusts: but follow righteousness,, faith, charity, peace, with them that call on the Lord out of a pure heart. But foolish and unlearned questions avoid, knowing that they do gender strife's. And the servant of the Lord must not strive; but be gentle unto all men, apt to teach, patient, in meekness instructing those that oppose themselves; if God peradventure will give them repentance to the acknowledging of the truth; and that they may recover themselves out of the snare of the devil, who are taken captive by him at his will." 2 Timothy 2:22-25

Let's recap again: The work of God in sanctifying the believer finishes with everlasting security in eternal life. To *qualify* for the beginning of sanctification one must be born-again. That is our part. Then God's *duty* is to sanctify you because He is your all powerful, all knowing, and ever-present supporter in the process of Sanctifying the saved-by-grace. Because of this He knows your capabilities and knows how to make you into the best you, that you can be. You are inhabited with the Holy Spirit who will counsel and guide you for the rest of life on earth. The saved-by-grace is forever <u>secure</u> in this mighty Love of Jesus and is at Peace with God.

Oh death where is your sting,–
oh grave where is your victory?
1 Corinthians 15:55

The earthly death of a Christian lands them in Heaven – Glorified! To be absent from the body, is to be present with the LORD.

RAP = Read And Pray

Relationship vs. Fellowship

During the sanctifying of our souls we learn the difference in relationship and fellowship. Sanctifying begins by the new birth and the entire objective to our growth as a Born-Again believer, saved by grace, is to learn how to fellowship with God. That is what He is after as He never stops pursuing our entire being. Sure, we belong to His family forever from that point, but He wants to give us the greatest of all blessings that is to be in fellowship with Him.

Our pastor at Eastside Baptist Church in Jasper, Alabama is Jeff Allred. He and his wife attended a Pastors Retreat at the Billy Graham training center located in Asheville, Tennessee. As with most conferences (that I have attended) a person comes away with one sentence or maybe even one word that grabs the heart for ponder-sake. I have found that (for me) most memorable sentence or word comes with a correction of some sort. It comes in a way of letting me know that I can do better, maybe even confess a sin, or learn how to regain focus on my true purpose of life.

The first Sunday home from this conference, Bro. Jeff preached a dynamic message that is included, with his approval, on the following pages. It is most fitting to be added in this session concerning Sanctification because all during our walk with the Lord on earth, we hit potential roadblocks, hurdles, and darkened valley in our journey. While we are working on our relationship with God, He also will teach us how to be in fellowship with Him, every day. In the following message you can see how relationship works and lead to abundant and glorious fellowship. After all, **_fellowship_** has always been what God truly wants with His children.

Ponder these two questions as you reflect on your own current relationship with God.

1. Do you have a healthy and thriving relationship with God?

2. Are you in constant Fellowship with Him?

RAP = Read And Pray

"There is a Difference Between Relationship and Fellowship"

<u>May 5, 2024 – Jeff Allred</u> (used by permission)

My wife and I have just returned from a conference at "The Cove" that is the Billy Graham Training Center. The keynote speaker was Jim Cymbala for the four days we were there. From the first day we had medical concerns with family members to the point of having to decide if we needed to return home or if we should stay. The worship with other pastors and their wives from all over the United States coupled with the praise and worship time was beyond words to explain. It was feeding our souls, yet we had to decide where we were needed most. We stayed and it was the last day and last message a phrase spoken hit me between the eyes and pierced my heart.

God understood the degree of my busyness in being a bi-vocational pastor, shepherding His flock while also studying and preparing messages, visiting and everything else that a pastor is called upon to be a part of. The words were:

> "Pastors, Your first calling is to be in <u>*fellowship*</u> with God."

As I was thinking about this on our drive home while my wife was sleeping in the passenger's seat, the Lord put this message on my heart. I have not prepared an outline for a power-point message, this one comes directly from my heart. I have asked myself if I have cheated on my church as your pastor and if I need to apologize to you for the recent messages concerning (1) The Message, (2) The Mission, and (3) The Ministry? Have I been too busy caring for you and preparing to deliver messages that I have neglected my fellowship with God? Let me explain how to grow fellowship.

God comes first. He is before all else if we want to grow and prosper in His will and be productive in delivering *His Message*, making it *His Mission*, and being used in *His Ministry*. We must first be in fellowship with Him. Sure we have relationship with God as a Christian, but I ask: "do we have fellowship with Him?"

When I had to fill out my contact information on the new iPad handed to me at the doctor's office, it asked for my contact person. Since July 17, 1993, that person has been my wife. I could list her as my contact person because I have relationship and fellowship with her.

Relationship for such, is considered to be the person to whom you are connected to by blood or marriage. Fellowship in definition means partnership and having someone with whom you have communion. The relationship I have with my wife covers both relationship and fellowship. I cannot separate the two.

In a marriage if all you have is relationship and not fellowship, you are missing the joys connected to building a solid and good life. Likewise I have relationships with my daughter, extended family, friends, and Jesus Christ. To my daughter I am her dad, to my friends – I am a friend, but, to Jesus I owe my life and certainly should be in fellowship with God just as surely as Jesus was in fellowship with Him while He lived in flesh and blood.

Revelation 3:14 Jesus said: "And unto the angel of the church of the Laodiceans write: These things saith the Amen, the faithful and true witness, the beginning of the creation of God; v. 15 I know thy works, that thou art neither cold nor hot: I would thou wert cold or hot. So then because thou art lukewarm, and neither cold nor hot, I will spue thee out of my mouth." Don't be guilty to think you have never made God so sick to His stomach that He didn't feel like vomiting. Perhaps, He would say, 'where is your fellowship with me'? Do I live so closely with you that you walk, talk, and listen in My presence'? Are we really in close fellowship with the One who bled on the Cross to give us eternal life?

The problem with the Laodiceans was that they were so independent, there was no fellowship with God. What about you and me? Even while sitting in church the mind wanders to where to go for lunch or a multitude of other things. Heart worship and praise is hindered because our fellowship with God is elsewhere. Revelation 3:20 Jesus said: "Behold, I stand at the door and knock: if any man hears my voice, and open the door, I will come in to him, and will sup with him, and he with me." Jesus said in John 21:12 – "Come and dine." The invitations to fellowship with God are endless.

Because of the fellowship between Jesus and His disciples, they knew what to do next. They were inside each other's lives. They walked together, lived together, and ate together. They fellowshipped. When we fellowship with God every day, then we know what to do next. The disciples recognized how much Jesus loved them.

In Ephesians chapter five you will find that the Bible teaches wives to submit to their husbands, and for husbands to love their wives as Christ loves the Church. This kind of submission means to submit with respect, honor and voluntarily. That is turn the husband is commanded to love their wives as Christ loves the Church. In this type of marriage, it is easy to recognize how much you are loved.

Our relationship with The LORD is the same. We can have relationship with Jesus and neglect the fellowship. The things that contribute to this cold and indifferent relationship are easy to spot. Idle busyness is around every corner. We take comfort in knowing we are saved forever, but absolutely miss the true joys of life with thoughts of bitterness, anger, hurts, sin, neglect, unforgiveness, disobedience, and worldly influence. Just to name a few. If we are too busy doing the work of the Message, Mission, and Ministry to fellowship with God; then the efforts of the Message, Mission, and Ministry fall short. Above all else we must be in fellowship with God. Give Him time, sit in His presence, enjoy His company. Let Him know you love Him.

Consider Jonah when He was out of fellowship with God, what happened? He ran in the opposite direction! The same thing happened to the prodigal son who left the good life for the wasteful life of self-indulgence. Then there is also the example of David with Bathsheba. While David stood idly on the rooftop sin was conceived and acted upon. In this wrong choice of lustfulness, David broke four of the Ten Commandments. He *coveted* another man's wife and *stole* her to commit *adultery* and ultimately *murder*.

Sin is not ok – it separates us from fellowship with God! Consider the contrast between Psalms 32 and Psalms 51. What happened after David's sin with Bathsheba? His silence (no fellowship with God) made his very bones "wax old". (32:3) He "dried up" (32:4). What God intended was vibrancy, victory, and fluency. David's actions resulted in a miserable, wretched dried up human being who did not confess until his hand was called by the prophet Nathan.(2 Samuel 12) There was no relief for David until he confessed and repented. Then he said: "Have mercy upon me. O God, according to thy loving kindness: according unto the multitude of thy tender mercies blot out my transgressions. Wash me thoroughly from mine iniquity and cleanse me from my sin." (Psalm 51:1-2)

David did not sin because of a bad heart condition (for he was a man after God's own heart) – David sinned because he was out of fellowship with God. His lustfulness took over and left him dried out.

RAP = Read And Pray

"Lord, forgive us for our idle busyness! You are more concerned with our "being" than our "doing". Lord, we need You, every hour we need you!

David is a true example of how God will never leave us or forsake us. He wants to cleanse us from all our sin and there is no sin that God cannot forgive. Fellowship with God can be restored. We should always give of our best to the Master because we need Him – oh how we need Him!

Mark 12:29-30 says: "And Jesus answered him, The first of all the commandments is, Hear, O Israel, The Lord our God is one Lord: And thou shalt love the Lord thy God with all thy heart, and with all thy soul, and with all thy mind, and with all thy strength: this is the *first* commandment." Notice this verse includes, the heart, the soul, the mind, and the strength of the body. Nothing is left out. All our being needs to be in fellowship with God every hour of the day. When we seek God we shall find Him ready and willing to restore us to true fellowship with Him. He will speak to us, dine with us, and yes, - fellowship with us.

Soak in the words of the old hymnal "I Need Thee Ev'ry Hour" (Mrs. Annie S. Hawks, Rev. Robert Lowry – sang by Chris Tomlin)

"I need Thee ev'ry hour, Most gracious Lord; No tender voice like Thine, Can peace afford, I need Thee, O I need Thee, ev'ry hour I need Thee! O bless me now, my Savior, I come to Thee! 2. I need Thee ev'ry hour, Stay Thou nearby; Temptations lose their pow'r When Thou art nigh. 3. I need Thee ev'ry hour, In joy or pain; Come quickly and abide, Or life is vain. 4. I need Thee ev'ry hour, Most Holy One; O make me Thine indeed Thou blessed Son! I need Thee, O I need Thee, Ev'ry hour I need Thee! O bless me now, my Savior, I come to Thee!"

Come to Jesus. Have fellowship with Him!

Jeff Allred
As told by Brenda Kendrick

RAP = Read And Pray

Glorification

<u>To be glorified by entrance into heaven means:</u>*"Joy unspeakable and full of Glory, away from sin and forever at peace with God".* Not just for a couple days, weeks, months, or years but rather eternally secure in the presence of our Savior, Jesus Christ *forever*. It also means being on the pinnacle of holiness with great satisfying contentment and uninhibited worship and praise. Glorification requires elevation from what was to what is. To be literal glorification means being absent from sin and its effects upon daily life. Forever in a place where sin cannot touch the core of your soul because your soul is totally Holy. Wholly Holy! While being sanctified one is called to be holy in an unholy world. When glorified one no longer lives in a sinful world and is therefore wholly holy.

Another point to consider concerning the eternal life of your soul is this: "God created you in your mother's womb and placed an eternal living soul in you at the same time. When that soul takes breath on its own, you became carnal (fleshly/sensual). You are still secure in God until you are capable of being accountable for yourself. Then a choice must be made. One may choose to be redeemed by the Blood Sacrifice of Jesus Christ, or not. The better choice, of course, is to receive Jesus as your atonement, but you will never be forced to obey God's plan.

The living soul within you *will live forever*. It cannot die. Why? Because when God breathed life into Adam and He became a living soul – all born after will also have that one breath because no part of God will ever die. This includes your soul. Therefore, one enters into life as an *eternal* being. Living in eternity from creation. If then, the soul within you will never die it is vitally important that one chooses heaven as their eternal home. Otherwise, the soul that rejects Christ, also rejects God and cannot live in His presence in Heaven. What is the alternative? A four-letter word, called 'hell' where all is miserable agony for eternity. It is only while living in the flesh that we have opportunity to decide where we will end up.

To be glorified is when God removes a person from a sinful world into a place where there is no sin and this ultimate transformation occurs when Christians enter into their eternal life in the presence of God in a place called heaven.

Glorification is the crowning achievement of sanctification. Instead of being mortals burdened with a sin nature, we will be changed into holy immortals with unhindered access in the kingdom of God. Glorification culminates in our restoration and transformation, both physically and spiritually and our bodies will be perfected, rejoined with soul and spirit in resurrection, and we will share in God's glory throughout eternity.

RAP = Read And Pray

References:

Read Romans 8:18 and 2 Corinthians 4:17 which emphasizes the removal of sin and the eternal state.

Read 1 Corinthians 15:51 which describes the instant transformation at the last trumpet.

Read 2 Corinthians 3:18 which speaks of believers being transformed into Christ's image from one degree of glory to another.

Read Psalm 104:2 describes God as clothed with splendor and majesty.

Read 1 Corinthians 15:35-54 where the apostle Paul discusses how the resurrected body is raised imperishable, in glory, and in power. He talks about Jesus' own resurrection which serves as a model, and how Christ's tomb was empty signifying His resurrection in the same body He had before death. Jesus' resurrected body represents our ultimate hope—a spiritual, imperishable, and glorious form that awaits believers in heaven.

Jesus is our Standard of Glorification

*"These words spake Jesus, and lifted up His eyes to heaven, and said, "Father, the hour is come; glorify thy Son, that thy Son also may glorify thee: as thou hast given Him power over all flesh, that He should give eternal life to as many as thou hast given Him. And this is life eternal, that they might know thee the only true God, and Jesus Christ, whom thou hast sent. I have glorified thee on the earth: I have finished the work that thou gavest me to do. And now, O Father, glorify thou me with thine own self with the glory that I had with thee before the world was. I have manifested thy name unto the men that thou gavest me out of the world: thine they were, and thou gavest them me; and they have kept thy word. Now they have known that all things whatsoever thou hast given me are of thee. For I have given unto them the words that thou gavest me; and they have received them and have known surely that I came out from thee, and they have believed that thou didst send me. **I pray for them**: I pray not for the world, but for them that thou hast given me; for they are thine. And all mine are thine, and thine are mine; and I am glorified in them. And now I am no more in the world, and I come to thee. Holy Father, keep through thine own name those whom thou hast given me, that they may be one, as we are."* John 17:1-11

RAP = Read And Pray

Finally, read how the entire book of John explains in vivid detail the work of Glorification and the Help of the Holy Spirit in Sanctification. This is most important to successful living in today's world. As we get closer to the rapture, it is increasingly important to believe the truth and teach the truth concerning salvation in Jesus Christ and the growth in intimacy with God through prayer and Bible study.

This is why the topics of Redemption, Justification, Sanctification and Glorification take up such a large part of these RAP session guidelines. Knowledge is only knowledge without application. What good is it to know how and why and not put those how's and why's to daily living?

Take some time to meditate on what **redemption, justification, sanctification and glorification** means to you then express your thoughts by creating your own outline of each topic or writing those thoughts and understanding of each on the blank pages that follow. You may also draw your thoughts if you prefer.

RAP = Read And Pray

Write out the meanings of the words below - in your own words:

Redemption is:

Justification is:

Sanctification is:

Glorification is:

RAP = Read And Pray

Your Notes and Comments:

RAP = Read And Pray

Summary
The Main Things

RAP = Read And Pray

The Main Thing
The Main Truth
The Main Love
The Main Victory

RAP = Read And Pray

The Main Thing

Jesus is The Main Thing. He is and has always been God's Crowning Glory and is the central being in all of history. He is God Almighty and Jesus is the only way for sins to be forgiven in order to become adopted into *The Family of God*. He alone made it possible for sin to be forgiven. Forgiveness of sin does not come from a Priest or Pastor or any other creature or created thing. Peace of God begins with God in human form, that is by way of Jesus Christ, His Son. No one is redeemed with corruptible things, but only by the precious blood of Christ, who was without blemish or spot. There is only one door into heaven – Jesus Christ opens that door because He is the Door. Jesus was more than a carpenter who built tables. He takes broken pieces of humanity and builds each one into His likeness. As He was a human but humble servant, so must we be. There is a date of birth, a date of salvation and a dash – followed by the final date of life on earth.

Let's review that one more time. A date of birth, a date of salvation and a dash. Then death on earth. Mine looks like this:

Date of Birth (DOB) July 31, 1951. Date of Salvation (DOS) April 21, 1978. (–) dash (my life span). Date of Death (DOD) Death date yet to be determined and doesn't matter because I already have Eternal Life in my Soul. Destination Heaven.

If I didn't know salvation in Jesus Christ then my history/legacy would not have two birthdates. It would simply look like this:

DOB/DOD July 31, 1951. Period. Destination 'hell'.

I would already be dead in the sight of God's Holiness that would separate me from Him - forever. The reason being we are born into eternal life for destination yet to be determined by CHOICE as to where It will live hereafter. All Souls live forever. Some choose Jesus Christ as their redemption, some do not. Sinful Souls cannot stand or live before The Holy God and The King of Kings.

What IF? What if everyone who has a tomb stone were required to enter two birthdates and only one date of death (which they would have to allow someone else to put of the tombstone for them). They could do nothing about that because they are dead. Wouldn't we be in a pickle? Imagine the chaos. Relatives would be running around asking each other whether or not the relative who died was a Christian. Otherwise they would not know what second date to put on the tombstone. This is futile because those who are Christians should live in such a way where no one would have to ask.

This brings up the second question: What about the people who know they are saved but can't remember the actual date to document. There is a difference in the words 'day' and 'date'. Those who are confident in their salvation will always remember *the day* even though they may forget the 'date' to record. People have a birth 'day' even though they may never

RAP = Read And Pray

celebrate the birth "date". I know I was born but if someone had not told me the actual date; I would never had known I was born on July 31, 1951. God records the rebirth 'date' while requiring us to remember the rebirth 'day'.

On my birthday I was present but at that point others took care of all my needs. On my rebirth day God took over that responsibility and became the One who would supply for all my needs. After my birthday I had to cry when I needed something because I could not yet verbalize what I wanted. After my rebirth day I still cried but God already knew what I needed. As an infant when my mother fed me, I was satisfied until the next time. As God's child when God feeds me with His Word He stays ever-present because He knows I will need more.

The same is true with some people who know that they know they are saved but can't for the life of them remember the actual 'date' it happened. They go through life thinking something is wrong or perhaps they are not saved. Take this comfort. No person has ever been saved without our Lord and Savior and God His Father telling the person. This has not and will not happen. That would be like me doubting I was ever born by my mother even though I can pinch my flesh and feel the pain. The Holy Spirit will not inhabit a person who doesn't belong in God's family.

The Main Thing in all of life is to know Jesus Christ as Savior of your soul. Period. The rest will be taken care of by God, your Father.

God knocks on heart. You know it is Jesus (the door) and a decision is made to either open the door or walk away. Suppose you walk away and never hear that knock again. God has done His part. Now suppose you open the door and Jesus walks in, gives you a big squeeze hug and pushes the door shut with His foot. From that time it is all hands off the door. Jesus is not going out. Would you say to Him – "Wait let me go right this *date* on the calendar so I won't forget it?" That would be absurd. He already has you in His arms and yall are dancing in the light of The Son. You are not about to forget that moment. You will never ever forget that moment in time. The calendar will flip to another month, then another year; but, that moment happened and is recorded on the time clock of your soul. More importantly, it is recorded in Heaven's Book of Life. That is comfort and everlasting peace.

The person who has never had such an experience is dead even while living, and that person has missed the best of the best of life on earth. Such a person has been a settler in all of their life's journey; settling for less when there is so much more. It's like choosing to eat the scraps from the floor instead of the banquet on the table. They settle for luck instead of miracles. That is such a shame! Not only has this person missed the truth of life, as God would have it, they also will miss heaven as well.

Have you ever wondered why God created us in His image? Maybe not, but I have. I'm a wonderer. I wonder how he told the oceans they could only come so far, and they obey?

RAP = Read And Pray

I wonder how He can only by His *word* cause a tsunami or, does He use the flip of His little finger to do so? I have wondered how the sun never burns itself out. I've even wondered when I look at my open hand how God knew I'd need a little finger. Oh, I could go on and on. Even in studying the Bible, there has been lots of things that left me wondering why and how? Even typing these alphabetical letters on this keyboard is a mystery to me that I even know how to put them together to forms words that hopefully you understand. Where does this knowledge come from? Who completely understands the things taken for granted? Do we actually tell our eyes to close and go to sleep or does our eyes tell us that we've had enough for the day? It is enough to drive a person slap mad!

When you have a God-given talent, God wants you to use it for His glory. Don't wait until your strength is almost gone to see this fact of life. A big regret in life is when a person gets old and realizes life could have been better if they had used these gifts and talents to advance God's kingdom.

That is why you must know what the <u>*main thing*</u> is. You are who you are because that is how God can get the most glory through your person and purpose. He absolutely knew what your strengths and weaknesses would be the day He delivered the soul within you. So quit wondering and looking in all the wrong places! Be the true you and that true you is a person who God wants in fellowship with Him. That is simply the one main thing that produces a happy and rewarding life on earth.

The Main Thing on earth is having that second birthday that comes in no other way but by being born-again into the Family of God through faith and trust in our Lord and Savior Jesus Christ. There is no other way to reach God and live in heaven someday. Quit trying to logically figure out life and its wonders. You don't have to know everything to know this one thing: - God spoke it all into being. We were created in His image, but His ways are not our ways. His ways are always the best ways. He gave us sense of choice for a reason. The mind who chooses God, does so willingly – never by force. The main thing of life is not: Getting, Going, and Doing

The Main Thing is always about JESUS.

RAP = Read And Pray

What is your *Main Thing*

RAP = Read And Pray

The Main Truth

After having received and accepted the Main Thing about Life – being and living in Christ Jesus – the truth of the matter is, being saved and missing hell is just the beginning of exploring *the main truth* in such a way that you live it every day and love to share that truth. However, we as humans, enter into our new life at various stages of our being.

Even though you are sealed for heaven that should not be your satisfying goal henceforth. Missing hell is something indeed that one should shout out loud to this deaf world; but there is something just as precious in the sight of God and that is to share that truth with others as He directs by the Holy Spirit.

Consider what would have happened to us here in 2024 had the Apostle Paul sat down after his conversion and decided "just missing hell is enough?" what if he thought – "I'm just going to live happy in my salvation and let others be blinded by God, then they will know how it feels." We would have missed almost half the New Testament that brings so much truth into a world of people satisfied with lies. Paul met Jesus Christ, was taught by Jesus Christ, and studied to know the truth. He journeyed far from where his mission and goal was to persecute believers and maybe even rejoiced in it like he himself had done God a service. Evidently he had enjoyed that way of life because he went out looking for even women and children to persecute and throw into prison for their beliefs.

My goodness gracious, don't you know Paul had to have had an encounter with Jeus Christ in order to flip his life and become a totally different human being? He called himself "the chief of sinners". He didn't need to grab a handwritten date keeper and circle that date, as you might when you log-in to your IPAD calendar. He remembered it explicitly because he was there when it happened; and so was Jesus. From that time he became the student who needed a teacher. He couldn't just go out and teach what he didn't know. He didn't know what he didn't know – until he knew what he didn't know. Once he knew – he did something about it. He taught it to others. A missionary of all missionaries was in the making.

Ask any born again Christian where they learned the truths about Christian living after being saved. It had to come from *God's Word*. And just how can we get God's Word? God instructed Paul to write the books of Romans, First and Second Corinthians, Galatians, Ephesians, Philippians, Colossians, First and Second Thessalonians, First and Second Timothy. Titus, and Philemon. Each of these as well as the other books of the New Testament were written by God-instructed, Holy-Spirit-dwelling writers of the New Testament who recorded the truth. If God used Paul to teach the truth, he had to have learned it somewhere. Right? He certainly didn't live it until he knew it and obeyed it.

Likewise, we cannot expect to live life to the fullest if we find a good thing such as salvation and decide to keep it to ourselves; satisfied to just miss hell. God forbid! Why? How can

RAP = Read And Pray

a Christian be satisfied with keeping all those nuggets and gems in a safe as if they didn't exist when the world needs to see the fruits of salvation?

Truth has a way (or at least should have a way) of coming out in a court of law. Do Christians keep silent because there is not enough evidence to convict them of being a Christian? For those who just want to make a change in their life, they invest nothing toward truth by just seeking a seemingly successful minister to follow – blindly. Run as fast as you can away from a teacher/preacher who teaches/preaches by opinion and does not feed you with The Scripture – The Word of God. Do not follow such. All that happens will be a feel-better-about-myself religion. That is not salvation and not God's Way.

God's way is the truth-way. And what is the truth? Jesus Christ is the truth. He is also the way and the life. Not, the death – but The *Life*!

God wants us to investigate Him and to investigate God starts with knowing His Son. Jesus introduces us to God and brings us into God's presence as a relative. A relative who is welcome at God's table to fill up for the journey ahead.

One more point here about knowing the truth. We cannot counsel God with our opinions. Isn't that ridiculous to even think we have enough wisdom to suggest to God that our opinions are better than His truths? He was in all yesterdays, in today, and already been in all tomorrows. He sees what we can't. He knows what we don't. He has power over all things. Then why is it so hard for us to trust Him with every single detail of our lives? Is it because we are not settled in the facts of truth because our opinions take precedency?

There are times when we need to put all our opinions on the table – rake them off onto the floor and sweep them out the door. Then, sit at the table with God and let Him set the table with His truth that is the meat of His Word. This is what Jesus was talking about when He instructs us to 'eat His flesh'. All things are about Jesus. Jesus alone can satisfy the hunger for in our hearts for truth. He is the **Main Thing** and He is the **Main Truth**.

The source of Truth is always JESUS.

RAP = Read And Pray

What is your *Main Truth?*

RAP = Read And Pray

The Main Love

When children leave the home of their main love-source and start school they seek acceptance and love among the new people who come into their circle. A shy girl may send a note asking a certain someone "do you like me? If you do then I like you too." Then leave a request to circle "yes" or "no" and send the note back. It seems this logic never stops. We want to be loved first before we commit and be sure the object of our love loves us back. We want relationships based on this theory in hopes of eliminating the pain of rejection. Knowing this is a fact of life, then why is it so hard for people to believe in God and accept Jesus Christ as life's security since He definitely loved us first? And going a step further – promises that He will always love us unconditionally, - no matter what.

There is no need to play this game with God because God always loves first. His delight in creating humans in the first place must have been in order to have that fellowship with them. And His greatest delight would be when they sincerely loved Him back.

Truth is, *nobody knows how to love until receiving the Giver of Love*. Once received one can give. No one can give that which they have never received. That's pretty simple logic. Compare agape love with the kind of forgiveness that chooses not to think on or even remember the offense: Total love vs: total forgiveness is not a competition where one or the other has to win. It's a package deal. We are all required to love and forgive. The strength to accomplish this victory comes only from God Almighty and victory in Jesus. God not only loves first, but He also loves forever. God not only forgives the sinner, but He also continues to forgive the sins. This process is done through our sanctification. Be honest, isn't this the most beautiful experience in all of life?

Knowing God loves you and has forgiven all your sins is true freedom and liberty. It is the approval slap on the back that says, "you are prepared to face the world now, go to it!"

The freedom to experience the goodness of life is eternal. Don't wait until you get to heaven to enjoy yourself. You can do that right here in the here-and-now. As a matter-of-fact God expects you to do just that with confidence that someone always loves you, has your back and will guide you through all unknown, with confidence in Jesus' keeping power. If I had to go through life afraid I was going to mess up then I'd be scared to death all the time and not go or do. What about you?

As I have confessed so many times before, I served God for a long time before I loved Him. That confession is flawed in that it is not true. Truth is, I was serving myself and others, not God. Any service done (for) God outside the realm of loving Him and obeying Hm – is nothing short of pure selfishness. God knows the motive. God sees the intent. He is not pleased with service which is not motivated by love. He wants us to quit playing Church and start loving Him with our entire being. That is what pleases Him, - then service will come and yield its benefits.

RAP = Read And Pray

I imagine God laughs at the thought of half-forgiveness or that people think this-or-that is beyond His scope of forgiveness. If He forgives totally then he can help us see the dangers of our superficial forgiveness. Although forgiveness is a two-way street sometimes one lane is closed. Roadblocks of denial can be set up causing detours that last a lot longer than they should. One side may be full of pitfalls and pot-holes while the other street is doing regular maintenance that drains resources, energy and time. Offers and good intentions go unanswered and unwanted.

Nevertheless, with God's forgiveness bestowed upon the offender, His grace is sufficient. He quickly says – "all is forgiven – go and sin no more." (Read John 8:1-11) The forgiven has the obligation to say – "thank you, thank you very much" acknowledge being forgiven, and accept it. No price to pay.

Saying "I'm sorry" is not complete until the offended says "You are forgiven." When and if you should be the blessed one who receives an apology after being attacked or hurt, don't miss the opportunity to let the apologizer know you accept the apology. Saying such not only frees oneself it also has the power to set the perpetrator free as well. The incident no longer separates you. Just like when our sins are forgiven we are no longer separated from God. However, let's get one very obvious thing uncovered here and now.

Earthly forgiveness is good for a person's health and wellbeing, but it does not erase the offense from heaven's record – *until* – the offender asks forgiveness from the actual ONE whom he offended. That being God Almighty. All sin offends God. It goes against Him and His ways. He hates sin so much that He cannot look upon it because He is totally Holy. Always has been and always will be.

God didn't just start loving a person when they were free from the penalty of everlasting death; He loved from the beginning – while all were sinners. What could make us think He would quit loving us when we sin? Would He have to send another Christ and shed more blood so we could be forgiven? That thought is a bigger insult to God than the first.

God loved us first and He will love us last. What happens in between is choice of fulfillment of His divine will or not. He never controls a loveless puppet; He embraces a loving soul.

That's what love looks like. The Main Love is always God's Love.

The Source of that love is always JESUS.

RAP = Read And Pray

What is your *Main Love?*

RAP = Read And Pray

The Main Victory

The victory for all team sports or personal challenge is what happens at the finish line, or the sound of the last buzzer. All cards played and all reserves exhausted. It is the moment of truth. Who wins? Who losses?

In the game of life (that is in fact not a game- but rather a purpose) the winners get to be **Glorified** while the losers finally have to recognize the truth by bowing a knee that previously refused to bend.

This victory is not because of personal strength but rather because in personal weakness God flexes His muscles and gives the strength to the meek and lowly. All Glory belongs to God and He does not have need of an earthly certificate, ribbon or trophy to display. He shows off the soul housed in a new body of His making. His Mansions are filled with the returned souls of those who chose to love Him back. However, these souls (me and you in celestial form) are not images set in stone to just look upon. We are finally freed of human limitation to worship God indeed like He deserves to be worshipped. Our heavenly bodies are consumed in expressing adoration, thankfulness, gratitude, praise and honor upon the giver of eternal life.

It will not be about what the mansion looks like or what jewels we receive. Heaven forbid. It will be about being in the presence of God Almighty, unashamed and unhindered in true flawless worship. Even after reading descriptions about heaven from the Bible I am at a loss to comprehend the beauty, peace and thrill of heaven because I am still being sanctified. So I concluded that heaven will begin when I am peacefully in the presence of my Savior – fearless.

The hands that were nailed to the Cross of Calvary will touch the palms of my hands. The hope and promise of eternity will then be a reality of being, seeing, and living forever. I know heaven is a real place even though I have not seen it – yet – because I know God created heaven and earth and I have already seen earth. (Read Genesis 1:1) The world He created for me to live in here on earth is extraordinarily magnificently incredible - so how much more will Heaven be? I'll just wait and see! Someday.

The question seemingly without an answer is what happens during the time a person is actually dying? Do they feel the suffering? Do they feel the joy?

I will leave you with a couple life-long visions that concern the moments of death. The first happened during the time my husband pastored a church and seemingly that called upon us to often be with families when their loved one passed away. Thankfully only once was it excruciatingly painful. Our friend's mother was on her death bed at home, and no one knew this lady's soul salvation. She had been fraying about and obvious distress but not verbal for many days. We witnessed this and it troubled our hearts. It was a vision I choose not to dwell upon. Her decision time had seemingly passed, and she seemed to be trying to

RAP = Read And Pray

get away from something. It was torture for the family who was powerless to help. I cannot give any more details on this situation for only God knows.

Then, I'll share the last moments of my father-in-law life on earth. We were at his bedside for days and somehow his eyes always seemed to be open even when he appeared to be asleep. He also could not talk. His greatest regret was having waited so long to be saved later in life rather than sooner. His eyes were cloudy so much so that it was hard to tell what color they were. I was on one side of his bed and my husband on the other and this is what I saw. *In one blink*, those eyes cleared, and I saw the blue sparkle. And I mean really sparkle! To you that may seem insignificant or no big deal; but to me it was evident that he had actually passed through death into eternal *life*. He was gone, peacefully.

Then not so long ago our family loss two relatives unexpectedly. My nephew was murdered and my granddaughter died in an automobile accident. In both these incidents, I was not present to see the end. Thinking about the possibilities associated with physical pain in such cases can be torment for a person's soul. It helped to know that both my nephew and my granddaughter were Christians and that I would see them again but it was still painful for us to deal with.

Then God gave me a dream.

I was in my earthly form and about to leave this life as well. I was in a vehicle that left the road and I saw certain death that no one could escape. I waited for the impact but there wasn't one. I felt myself flying through the air and I saw the trees passing by as I went through them without being hit by any one of them. I didn't even dodge to miss them. It was just a very peaceful moment as I watched it unfold. At a time when I should have been mangled and feel the pain of death; I didn't. Even in the dream I had reasoning enough to know I should be dead, but I did not feel the sting of it. I woke up and that is all I remembered about the dream.

Does this mean God gave me a vision to witness how I might die? No, I don't think so. I believe He gave me this vivid dream as assurance to what I already knew. There is no fear and no pain in the death of a redeemed person. No matter how a person may die, they will not live to totally explain it to you in any way that you might understand. And, that is alright. Because for a Christian, life on earth is no longer where they desire to be. All because of Glorification.

For the Christian, at death the soul steps from one body into another and I believe there is no pain in the stepping. The soul just goes, in peace. This truth comes by revelation from God to the redeemed. It is not by intellect. That is enough to live on and die by. Have liberty. Be free. Don't be saddled with dread and doubt. Love life. Live life. God will handle the details.

RAP = Read And Pray

I am free. I have confidence in both living and in dying and that is victory. Not of my own doing in any form or fashion; but simply by the love of God and the grace found in Jesus Christ. I should spend my days thanking God that I know the main thing, truth, and love. For in those things there is victory.

To be successful in your walk with the Lord Jesus Christ – Keep your **Focus on God**.

The Main Victory is being in the presence of JESUS forever.

What is your Main Victory?

RAP = Read And Pray

Do not skip answering the questions listed in this section. By answering those four questions truthfully, it will become very obvious where you stand in your faith and spiritual growth as a Christian. Hopefully, now having points to ponder, it is up to every individual to align themselves with the truth, purpose and divine will of God.

What is God's will for you?

God's will is for each of us to live under His wing and always in the Light of His Love, trusting in His Son and to love, respect and honor Him by loving, respecting and honoring others. He is always in control and "Has You Covered".

> *But the wisdom that is from above is first pure,*
> *then peaceable, gentle, and easy to be intreated,*
> *full of mercy and good fruits,*
> *without partiality,*
> *and without hypocrisy.*
> James 3:17

RAP = Read And Pray
\

"The grace of our Lord Jesus Christ be with you all. Amen"

Revelation 22:21

Made in the USA
Columbia, SC
11 December 2024

49072632R00138